MEMORIES FROM THE END OF THE WORLD

Ewen MacDonald

HEDDON PUBLISHING

First edition published in 2018 by Heddon Publishing.

ISBN 978-1-9997027-7-9

Cover design by Catherine Clarke

Book design and layout by Katharine Smith,
Heddon Publishing.

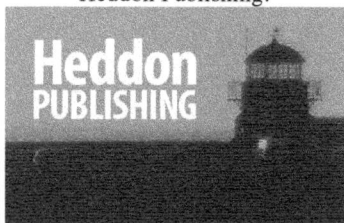

www.heddonpublishing.com
www.facebook.com/heddonpublishing
@PublishHeddon

For Luka

To whom I would give the world

Born and raised in the Scottish Highlands, Ewen MacDonald has also been a resident of Inverness, the Isle of Skye, the Channel Islands and Leicester. He has a degree in history and has also studied film, photography and architecture.

Throughout his career, he has variously been an electrician, civil servant, trade unionist, general factotum, plongeur, and, for a brief spell, a gallerist. He currently works as a freelance writer and photographer. He is married with one son and lives in Cornwall.

It was his pulse he could feel, gradually rejecting his body. It was now just a muted yawn through the valves of his heart. It would tighten, then stop, and the universe would cease to be.

It had happened a long time before, the nine-month gestation period, of which you had never felt a part. A distant event which had held such a momentous consequence for you. More so for you than anyone else. Your mother could have died, or she could have lived on, but she would always be separate from you; as separate as all the others.

Here he lies on the bed, surrounded by the expellants from his body. Just like when he arrived coated in his mother's placenta, an umbilical cord wiring loosely through the impenetrable space between the womb and the hospital ward. He is dying now, at one and apace with the former self screaming into the daylight. Yet now he groans imperceptibly towards the night.

His throat is parched and hollow. His bones wither away from the edges of the damp mattress. The lead paint in the yellow walls breathes out its moist and fungal breath. If only his tongue could release a ball of spit and roll it towards the back of his throat.

I am entering the end of my final day; a day which stretches back to that first which I can no longer remember. A fuck, in a banal bedroom; or perhaps a sun-blessed summer meadow. Genesis begins somewhere; it's a mere question of geography.

I cannot forge the time into an ellipsis to meet that small infant child. I cannot weld beginning and end to form an infinite junction.

It is here I shall expire. A disintegrating bed, in an ancient village which I have no name for. The man inside of this crepuscular husk is being methodically erased. Yet the rudiments are still glinting behind the frozen veneer of an impenetrable death mask.

The mosquito which scours the room ceaselessly is pregnant with its diseased blood. The voluminous load with which the vampiric insect hovers above its quarry is primed to explode across the cement walls.

He cannot raise his arm to swat the tormentor, gluttonous and unfulfilled, who strafes his skin at will.

The dark heat of the desert savannah enters through the small, bright opening in the wall by his bed, banishing all hope of a mild relief. In the morning, a young woman had tenderly washed his feet with tepid water and left a cool, damp cloth on his head, which had quickly turned feverish from sweat. She had smiled gently at him and cooed a hush at him to comfort his despair.

The dry, sulphuric scent seeps through the rotted, wooden flooring. Out on the dusty plains there is carrion stripped to the bone. Some rotting morsels of flesh remain, their stench wafting along on the wisps of parched winds. It is the remnants of a decaying death, picked over by predators and scavengers alike, which he smells. The singeing sting of the desert heat mixed with the warm, festering blood of the freshly butchered carcass. The sun burns everything in this landscape: the people; the houses; the cattle, and the earth beneath the soles of the feet.

I long for the rain of home. How it washed the leaves from the trees in the autumn and sludged them around the edges of the grey, despairing pavements. They too smell of decay, of an innocence grindingly slipping away.

And yet to feel the bracing shock of a polar breeze slapping my face one more time, before I descend through that mysterious abyss on the black outskirts of time.

The cows can be heard lowing in their scrubby pasture. Their heavy bells are clanking around their necks. You are dreaming of their faces, from the confines of your bed. They remind you of a photograph, of a big black staring eye, filled with a kind of sadness and melancholic foreboding. The photograph was titled *Off to the slaughterhouse*. The field the cow stood in was a verdant enclosure in England. Far away from where you lie now. The photograph triggers further associations of Warhol's cow wallpaper, which you viewed at Nottingham Castle; or was it at MOCA? When you stood outside on the street and gazed up at the sky. You felt that it was the bluest sky you had ever witnessed. The sun was a giant, white, raging furnace. A sun like they had in Athens: so different from the one in Moscow; or Tokyo, even.

I lie down on the sand on Venice Beach. I can hear the laughter and the music of the Pacific Ocean, calling to me even now. The waves lulling onto the sand on a windless spring day. I can feel her bleached, blonde hair touching my skin, her perfume and a little fresh sweat on her forehead, which mingle with her sun cream.

'Do you like it here?' she asked me. 'In the heat of the desert and the cool of the ocean? Isn't it really cold where you're from?'

'You don't mind it so much when you're young and you don't know any different. The summers seemed long enough back then. And we got the same movies and television shows as you. The colours just seemed brighter than we were used to, that's all,' I answered but she had escaped already, back into that endless blue in the sky.

The light in the room is fading: it creeps trepidatiously along the wall, clinging to its coolness. The light is fading inside me, too. There is nothing left onto which it can anchor itself. All those times in the past I wondered how I could unplug myself from this world, without arousing too much suspicion from those surrounding me. There it is now: it comes for me tonight.

The cataract of twilight is closing his eyes. The sun is lolling towards the horizon. Its fierce heat will end, then the humid hum of nightfall will commence. He will not breathe in the dusky heat of the new dawn.

There is a whisper in the dark that calls out to you. It is the voice of a woman: it is your mother. She is dead. They are all dead. You are the last of your kind.

'My son, you are expiring.'

It is not the voice of my mother. It must be the voice of another's. Calling through the blackness of that void. The darkness of the encroaching night. I can't see her face anymore. How long has it been? Have I imagined a face; the face of another? Can it have been her voice?

'Say nighty night, now it's time for beddie bye-byes.'

The herdsmen call their cattle to order and lay them down for the night. They will sleep amongst their beasts, tend them and watch over them. Their livestock will be safe from surrounding predators whose eyes sparkle malevolently in the dark of the night.

Something with hooves passes under the window. You think of the girl who used to ride past your house on the large, brown horse. Her white thighs, tightly gripping the black saddle. Her long red hair curling around her shoulders. You were fifteen years old; she was nineteen. You remember her face still, but you cannot remember her name. She seemed so imperious and unattainable as she moved through the square frame of your bedroom window.

Is she too dying this night? Or is it simply the memory of her?

The wild desert grasses flutter in the gentle breeze. Scorpions scurry from beneath hard stones as the creatures of the nocturne ready themselves for the nightly battle of their survival.

The fearsome heat will not fade much now that the sun is disappearing. The sweat will still cling to skin and sheets. The twilight will mask the landscape in a dreary, murky light; so different to the golden flames which ignite the soil in a reddish haze during sundown.

It was the pinks of the sunrise yawning over the mountains in the springtime back home. Watching it from the small garden, standing in my pyjamas. My father joyfully extolling its beauty and the nature of the countryside in which we grew up.

'This is your land, son, the land of your fathers. They fought to keep it from the hands of the Romans, the Sassenachs, and the dreaded Nazis. Perhaps it's the most beautiful land in the world. And it belongs to all of us.'

Were there tears when he said it, or do I simply imagine them?

You search for the palate that has now vanished. A meal of *fabada asturiana* served piping hot in that little rustic tavern near Gijon. That deeply unctuous dish: the smokiness of the chorizo, the sweet spiciness of the morcilla, and that rich red stock.

How you wandered through those rain-swept mountains so beloved by Hemingway, on down through the plains of Castille, and eventually arrived in the parched earth of Andalusia, where you searched out the girls with the roses in their hair.

That sun-bleached land with its deep, dusky, earthy scents. The sun singeing and scorching the earth. The dusty remains of its hell filling the nostrils.

The dark has settled over the land. Strange sounds emanate from outside the little window. Two voices pass by, softly lulling their words in a language you don't recognise.

You went deep into the zone. The tormented bed, the enclosed white walls, the blinds all drawn and the dark-set winter outside. You sweated and churned and choked and vomited. You scratched at your veins to see if they might still bleed warmth. You cut a deep gash in your own forearm with a metal ruler. Your eyes couldn't focus and your brain couldn't function.

You tried to set out pictures in a sketchbook with a pencil, but they wouldn't form. The images had dissipated.

Delirious, you wept, filling the soft pillow with tears.

There was a hand-woven Afghan rug on the floor, which had passed through a carpet shop in Istanbul. Blood pooled in a little well in the centre of the rug as it dripped down through your fingers.

My brother lies horizontally in a metal bathtub, which is all shining steel. He is just a torso. His eyes are missing, they are deep pools of black. His mouth opens cavernously and hundreds of live sardines slither and tumble from it and begin ravenously to devour him.

The sweat curls down my back. I am a ruined, naked form on the floor. The sickness won't leave my stomach; it contorts and twists my innards, squeezing and rinsing them of life. My trembling hand can't grasp the piece of wood and graphite by my head.

I try to blow a wisp of fluff away from my face, but it won't budge. The owner will find me here; a decomposing lump of mottled human flesh.

I begin to urinate across the wooden flooring. The piss pools away from me then returns by way of an uneven board, drenching my penis and balls. Trying to find its way back to the source. It smells viscous and diseased, as though my being is trying to escape itself.

If I could grip the pencil and draw my outline, at least.

I had that feeling of death even then, as though its hand was gently gripping mine. It comes for me in earnest this night. Caressing me down into that unfathomable blackness. A swift bullet and then I would be no more. We suffer greatly in our endless, drawn-out game of waiting.

In the end they pile you into the pit of the earth on your own.

Nobody ever knew if you were faking it or not; the life you were choosing to live. A life of carefree hardships, of which you refused to endorse yourself.

I am dying and this is to be my final resting place. There is no need now to curse all the others. Any and every other who could be held responsible for my ailments and my predicament. It is I alone. It was always I, who is me in myself, wrapped in my shroud of solitary anonymity. It is I who has lived and it is I who shall die.

It was death that you witnessed in that car. Your childhood friend slumped over in the driver's seat, with a broken neck. His colourless eyes staring out past you and into his own tender grave. A skid on the ice and a large pine tree ended your winter's evening journey.

On the crumpled blue metal of the bonnet you watched a fresh flurry of white snow pile up. Then you passed out in the passenger seat with a fracture in your left femur. The fire crew cut you free and the ambulance crew sped you to hospital. You were still in your ward bed when his coffin was silently slipped into the freshly-dug frozen earth.

The snow sways tenderly on the crushed car. White and blue serenely knitted together. I say his name, garbled into that sad abyss which now passes between us. The pain wells deeper and sharper and I cry out for my own suffering. His pains have ended. I want to touch him once more, reach out in quiet comradeship for all our past associations. My pal, my now dead pal. His life robbed of sixty years and more.

The sounds of the night whisper into his pitch-black room. There can be heard the occasional stirring of a cow in the dusty, hot scrubland, and the wilting humour of the herdsmen as they bed down to sleep.

The approaching nightly breeze whips grains of hard sand up into the gloomy, heavy air. Outside in the dark, they try to protect themselves against the harsh, gritty debris. He, too, averts his eyes under a stained and moist white sheet.

That listlessness which drains me now was ever my foe. A *bête noire* waiting around the crack of dawn to devour my scrawny skeleton.

I scaled that great hill, beyond our house, every July of my childhood. From out in the landscape I imagined I could spy the rolling shore break of the Atlantic Ocean. That tide which would carry me off to the new world: to hope and adventure and freedom. The sea, though, was too far in the horizon to ever be viewed from that short summit.

I can still feel my spindly, sunburned legs moving through the cancerous bracken and flowering heathers, to wrest the joyous celebration in my heart at having climbed all the way to the top. To lean back on the warm, brown grasses and pick out my house nestled deep below, on the steeply sloping hill.

The deep, rustic red of the earth has disappeared into a vague topographical canvas punctuated by a wide brimming nightscape: its carapace the sparkling of a million spinning stars. The embers of a fire gently extinguish themselves, sending the final wisps of smoke out into an infinite landscape of desert sands and scrublands.

When we were young we played down by the banks of the dark, mysterious river. Deep and cavernous, raging with trout and salmon, and with bridges that spanned it and rapids which flowed through it. We dug large pits in the sand and covered them over with corrugated iron and bushes and we sat inside and read comics.

The underlay of sand was cold against our backs so we fitted in old, discarded carpets as a form of comfortable furnishings. We laid an old rubber hosepipe between the two foxholes and communicated with each other back and forth.

We are there in the semi-light seeping in through the cast-out hole above us. We talk among the shadows, in a pit in the earth. If a boat should glance along the shore, we do not exist. We are secreted in the sand, by the gentle lisping of the river washing over the shore we have carved ourselves among. The last of our childhood creaking towards adolescence and the turbulence and tribulations of a wider ocean.

'The Bash Street Kids are really good this week. I wish I could draw like that,' I say.

'It says here, in this magazine, that sharks have two penises.'

'Two?' I ask. 'What do they need two for?'

'Don't know. Maybe they can shag two female sharks at the same time,' he concludes.

The stars can almost be heard from inside this humid stone mausoleum, as though their cosmic vibrations are travelling down through the universe to call the dust particles back into their infinite womb. That most desperate of our desires, for a return to the mothership. To once again be reduced to a single-cell organism: a being in itself.

I will soon enough be one with the earth and the harsh sand grains of this desolate landscape. A dark-clad reaper will creep through the hole in the wall and reclaim my soul for an eternity of damnation, or perhaps even salvation. We shall both stealthily seep from this black sarcophagus into the incandescent red of the new dawn.

In the wintertime, under a firm blanket of snow, you awoke to find the inside pane of your bedroom window encrusted deep with frost. A frozen veneer too thick to simply wipe off with a cloth. You would hold the steam of your warm, sweet, milky tea up to the glass and watch the ice transform into pools of water on the cracked wooden windowsill. From there, it trickled down the woodchip wallpaper peppered with black spores of dampness.

I am in warm, light surroundings. I cannot place the geographical location, nor a sense of space. Wherever this place is, it appears to exist on its own plane. 'You are here,' Our Lady tells me. She is beautiful and benevolent and dressed in blue and white. She smiles serenely at me. 'It's okay, you are in heaven.' I am too young to be dead. My parents will be angry. She recedes. The vision disappears. It disappears forever.

He shifts himself in bed in a clockwise fashion, the tattered pillow remaining defiantly beneath his oozing skull. His weakened vocal chords make a tremulous rattle as the agony of the movement passes through his crumbling bones. His calcified fingers grip the tattered sheet with all the strength they can muster. The thumbs tenderly caress the worn Egyptian cotton as he tugs away at the hem of death.

The true dark of the night offers me no relief. The heat clings to my skin and my soul. The moisture deepens the welts of regrets and sins. Heat carves in the memory those flashes of pure white brilliance, when life affords a passage back into the realms of our forgotten consciousness: after which death always discovers us.

I stand in the clammy haze of an unreasonably hot August, inside the sparklingly clinical surrounds of the newly cleansed Reichstag building. An old man, withered over, glances at the forgotten photographs of the NSDAP delegates to the assembly. He murmurs some words in German which I cannot understand. I shuffle surreptitiously closer and manage to capture the words *Meister* and *Deutschland*. I melodramatically take him for an ancient SS murderer, come to bid farewell to his fallen comrades and fellow gangsters, and to recite his creed to the new order of the thousand-year-old Reich. An order which was dead and buried and an empire which had crumbled into the dust and dirt of that vast tomb, Stalingrad.

Perhaps it is his perilous attempt to resurrect the demons, once vanquished, that they may forever stalk the darkness of the earth.

The soft and gentle tears which roll down the deep-set cracks of that old and worn face spell something different altogether. They speak of a thousand years and more of suffering, of defeats and humiliations.

My arm turns to meets his - to steady it - but he is gone, shuffling along, a young woman with long black hair by his side, to tender him comfort.

The dark seeps in through the pores in the walls. It fills the spatial void until it encompasses all of the universe and all eternity. The dust still shifts outside, pushing the dirt and grit up against the walls. The mild bluster of the relentlessly hot wind stealthily creeps in the window and caresses the stagnant, disease-riddled air surrounding him.

Lying in that room with the blinds drawn, perched on the upwards gradient of the hill, an elm tree rattling in the cold wind outside, you stared out for hours and then days, the fever burning within you.

Eating melting ice creams, cautiously retrieved, from the broken-down refrigerator in the kitchen next door. With a curious intensity, you licked the strawberry and chocolate down to the cone, which you then discarded on the floor. You urinated in the sink and every few days you traversed the stairs on all fours to defecate in the toilet bowl. Your skin was dry and your bones were skeletal. You ran your aching fingers over your naked elbows and hips, feeling every hard edge, as though the rigor mortis had set in already.

Where was the Bacon exhibition? There was that one in the museum of modern art in Edinburgh, or is it Paris that I'm recalling? George Dyer slumped over the toilet bowl. The Giacomettis were in the same room. I would have set up a bed in the centre of the space, with clean and crisp bed linen and a pair of brown leather slippers neatly tucked in underneath. No other distractions needed in such enduringly theatrical surroundings.

I could have lived in such an arena and set up house there. The dream of the grand apartment filled from room to room with great art and tastefully positioned icons of modernist design.

The opiate wastrel gliding effortlessly from one rock-and-roll binge of calamitous excess to the next. Stumbling through life as a beautiful corpse. A dandified demon endlessly exhaling sex and death.

He endures a soundless scream as he grips the sheet as tightly as his decrepit hand dares. Outside in the dark desert landscape, the glare of the moon is given full rein. It pierces and scratches its residue over the lunging heat of the deep sand carpet, leaving only a monochrome palimpsest in its wake.

His rictus supplications towards the doorway for some form of human warmth or comfort go unheeded. The world is silent and the universe has been emptied of all but the now dim light fading from his eyes.

The still, green pools are settled deep within the fissure in the mountainside. The blue sky, the white clouds and the light grey of the giant boulders are reflected in their cold, crisp jaws. We dive clear into them, foolhardy of their intensely frozen grasp. Those June waters bathed still in the fresh dew of the winter snows. Our heads emerge reborn: piercing through the glacial ripples with chattering teeth and clattering bones. We heave our shrunken bodies onto the warm, smooth stone, clasp our jumpers around us. Underneath the icy sweat is skin covered in goose bumps. That meek sun never felt so new, so inflamed, and so inadequate to the task at hand. Our baptismal joy at the first of the summer bathing complete, we leap back down the mountainside, springing ourselves from rock to rock.

You carried yourself down those streams and glens cautiously. Gingerly pacing your steps to keep abreast of the others, but never marking yourself agile enough to pick up on point. You observed closely how your friends fared in their footholds before venturing forth yourself. Their cries of encouragement echoing down the narrow cleft of stone.

'Hurry up, you dick.'

'Last one to the bottom's a cunt.'

'Up your arse, bastards,' comes your giddy reply.

The gradients were at times precipitous, the dangers in that wilderness myriad, but you stealthily navigated them all with the controlled awareness of an extreme sensitivity to survival and preservation of the self.

The heavens above are fully aglow with a nocturnal lighting display. Their transcendent musings perfectly encapsulate the hushed calm of the still night air. Its stifling heat quivers yet, but perception is everything in these lands and it benevolently lends a fluctuating coolness mingled in with its momentary pauses for inhaling breath.

The darkest outreaches of space filter down tenderly on the earth. A blanket of stars are held captive over the ever-expanding curvature of the desert's linear boundaries. Their arcing phosphorous glow highlights the demarcation of the horizon.

In several hours' time the soft morning light will engage the world again. I will not rise from my tomb here. Coiled in a fetid and torn bed sheet which will fall from me, I will enter into a separate state of being.

In the evening, with triumphant aplomb, the lightning crackled all over the sky in beautiful, tragic Berlin. We sat there, us two, and marvelled at its power and energy and its squandered majesty. We sat across from one another as the restaurant rotated high up in the Fernsehturm.

That pall of a humid August air hung low over the entire city until its raging fury burst down upon Alexanderplatz and Karl-Marx-Allee.

'Christ, that's some real lighting display,' I proclaim.

'Lightning frightens me,' you say.

'I'm sure we're safe enough. These buildings have always got lightning rods on their roofs. They're designed for it. This place is probably one giant lightning rod, earthed to the soil.'

'I still don't like it.'

'Well, you know how efficient the Germans are with engineering.'

I mean to comfort you. Tell you that I, too, am scared.

We watch the rats as they scurry through the park, in some blind, panicking attempt to avoid the torrent. Then we shelter under a bus stop and stare at the place where they had burnt the books all those terrible years before.

Trapped in that urban nightmare, you never felt so despairing. You told one another you would never conceive children. You would never conspire to keep the human race alive after such unimaginable crimes. And you turned to her and asked, 'How can we exist after Auschwitz?'

'I don't know,' she answered tremblingly.

In the mornings, the heat breaks open again and each day in this scorched land feels more incinerated than the day before. Each moment is more unbearable than the last. The body seeks out and clings to every ounce of shadow it can discover. Pinning itself to the walls of any which can shelter it. The light is so intense, it strips the landscape of all contours and all you can smell is the heat and the sand and the sweat flaking off from your burnt skin.

It is night but you perspire still in your linen coffin. Your parched breath cries out for water, but there is none to be had. The carafe is empty of its contents and it will not be filled again until daylight, when you will be dead.

When the snow fell at home it swept through the air in giant shavings: blanketing itself on the frozen ground. As children, we would run outside as quickly as our mittens and wellies would take us.

The hill we slid down. How far was it from the house?

We all gathered to take our turn and held a cheap plastic bag underneath us, and swirled and spun all the way down. The tough boys would always push us out of the way and take several turns after another.

'Out of the way, you wee sissy cunt.'

'Stupid fuckin' fanny. What are you gawping at?'

'Do you want a kick in the balls to warm them up, you big fat shite?.'

'Aww, he's gonna run home crying to his mammy, the fuckin' wee cry-baby bastard.'

I always hated them for it.

The cold; that biting, terminal, frost-encrusted cold. I can still feel the vaguest sense of plunging my hand into that soft, pure snow. The instant shock on the fingertips, the snapping of teeth together and the relief when the hand was set free again into the milder air.

When you went home again, crying with the painful numbness in your hands, your mother would rub them gently and breathe on them to defrost them. Then you would creak them open again in front of the warmth of the bars of the fire. Life finally returning into them.

The dripping gloves always on the radiator in the kitchen, drying. The snow from the boots always melting. Pools of grey water lay stagnant on the linoleum floor as the blanket of whiteness piled up further on the airless kitchen window.

The light had a pale, monochrome dullness to it as that cold, bleak darkness hung ever-present over the country. The streetlamps worked hard then: sixteen hours or more.

In the morning there was the wheezy breath sharp against the polar air as I rose from bed, my eyes bleary against the orange glow of the single light bulb. My mother must have woken me as my father slept on still. She didn't disturb him. He couldn't have had any work that week.

'Time to get up for school, son. Come on, you're late as it is,' she would chirp gaily.

I can't find the outline of my father's face anymore. His eyes were always so dark and haunted.

His body looks set for the grave already. It hardly knows now how to breathe, nor dares to, for fear of waking the ghosts which haunt his bedside. The eyes have glossed over: whatever soul there is will soon enough take flight.

They were hard of heart back then, beat us black and blue in those classrooms. Hadn't worked their way yet out of the Victorian mindset. All they seemed to want was silence and obedience.

She stands there with her long, curled red hair, freckles still on her face, even though she must have been in her early twenties at least. Her tight brown jumper accentuating her breasts, her blue jeans tight against her bum and rolled high up her calves, with the brown leather, high-heeled boots beneath.

'Put your hands out,' she commands. 'Both of them.'

She straps the boy across the palms of his hands with a leather tawse. Each lash louder and heavier than the last. She is cruel and she is gorgeous. I don't want her to hurt him. I want her to like me. I don't know why.

You never found it so easy. Worried that you simply did not have the constitution the others seemed to display. You weren't sturdy enough for the part. You couldn't take the punches the others were capable of taking. Eventually, you slugged your way through it all, but the defeats kept coming and they felt so endless.

The inner strength and resilience continued to waver, right up to the end. You watched as others battled courageously all the way through, but not you. They were flawed or fools, usurpers or cheats, witless or devious, pampered or pretentious, nepotists or plagiarists. They were anything at all, but they were not you.

Standing before it, in the hallowed seat of the papacy. There she was, beatific and sublime, holding her infant child: the Pietá. Carved from marble as a young man.

16

The serenity, the craftsmanship, the adulation, the utter impossibility of the task. And yet there it stood, the living proof; so beautiful and so tragic. I want to feel all of the folds of Our Lady's garment, the curls of Christ's hair. Between me and the sculpture lies the bulletproof glass.

You returned to your hotel room with the painting of Mary placed above your bed. You sat on the edge of the mattress and wept, because you knew it was no use. You could never attain such heights. In one thousand years of heavy travails you would never even come marginally close. Michelangelo was Michelangelo and you were you.

Sitting at the table in the hotel room, I closed my eyes and tried to sketch it out on a little pad. Find all the line I could. Discover all the detail. That youthful face and that languid body.

I did not sketch them, but myself and my mother. Momentarily, I was Christ: forgiving and redemptive. The powers of the heavens were blessed in me and in my pencil. Upon checking out, I left the sketch behind, along with a tip, for the chambermaid. Her dark hair and long nose. She was sweet and polite.

'*Grazie, signore.*'

'*Prego, signore.*'

'*Mi scusi, signore.*'

I wonder what she did with it. Laugh and throw it in the waste bin. Bring it home for her devout mother. A portrait of the artist as a Pietá.

What became of it within me? A large, framed drawing on a gallery wall. Self-portrait as the son of God. Supine, on a sinister-looking chaise longue. The detritus of my life around me: syringes, bottles, spliffs, pills, condoms, takeaway cartons, a sketch pad with a drawing of the Pietá in it.

You lie there too weak to complain any more, too wretched to comprehend your condition, too insane now to rationalise it all. The heat burns at your temples. Your throat and lungs are tinder. Your organs are all closing down.

The scythe moans throughout the night, cutting through any body contaminated by the stench of death. Its mask is held down low and its swing is true and strong. He lies there traversing the blankness of the walls with a tender terror of that impossible instant when his eyes will close for the last time.

We stood by the banks of the river. Several of us in a row. All watching that line cast out across the water's dark sheen, waiting for a tug on that float. It came calling for me only once. A foot-long, slippery eel, slapping around in the warm summer air. I couldn't disgorge the hook from its innards and so I swung it hard against a rock; three, maybe four, times. Still it would not die. Finally, I gutted it fully down its length with my trusted penknife. I suppose it must have died then, but I couldn't tell. I simply threw it back into the water, as carrion for the fish, with the hook still stuck in its gut.

'Look at the fuckin' state of that thing,' one of my pals laughed uproariously at the sight of the eviscerated eel.

'You couldn't even get a stray dog to eat that,' another interjected.

You watched the water and waited for the ripples to appear and the small pockets of air to rise to the surface, but they never came. The successful boys had marshalled themselves to a different part of the river. It belonged to them: it was their due. They were masters of the waterways, the true hunters, and the men who would survive. You were born to starve, unable to sustain yourself, your fate to eventually wither and die.

You saw the beauty in the river: its graceful, swirling body; its rages and its nonchalant meanders. The silver birches lining the banks were a source of great aesthetic joy to you and the fishing lines snaking out across the surface of the water, into the deepest recesses, were elegant marks cast out by human hands.

A silence booms across the desert terrain as infinitesimal grains of sand move marginally along their chaotic route, centimetres at a time, until they reach a destination hundreds or thousands of miles away. For now there is a hush, with the dominant night sky omnipotent, omniscient and omnipresent. The gentle moonlight illuminates the sand dunes and casts them as smooth gestural marks in the far distance.

He sleeps lightly: a rasping sound emanating from his rattling lungs. His mouth lies slightly ajar and his teeth are mortified forms of ruin. The shoulder and clavicle are already the fused elements of a decaying corpse. His skull rests on the pillow, an apparition of its former self. The eyelids feebly dressing the sunken sockets below. There is peace: a momentary truce with the world. A respite from the onward decay of the body corporeal.

A black space, a hollow with a willowy tree dancing on a minor breeze. The reductive noise of fear and terror gripping the veins. Down here there is no illumination, only varying shades of a deep blackness. A black so dark it borders on red. The hands attempt to grip the image: freeze it for eternity. There is no more palate. There are no more implements and tools with which to convey that inner sight. The body is too weak: a calcification all the way to the tomb. Only the mind can still envision the marks to be made.

You drew pictures on the first day of your pedagogic journey through childhood. They gave you coloured sheets of paper and coloured pencils. You drew a car and a tree and a house and your mother and your father and your brother and your teddy bear, Bobby.

You had been drawing since you could remember. A large pad of white sheets of paper and a pack of rainbow-coloured felt pens - tightly packed in a plastic pouch with a small plastic catch - that your aunt had bought you for your third birthday.

'I got these for him. I remember the last time I was here, he was so engrossed in his crayons.' Your aunt gazing benevolently down at you.

You immediately sat down at the kitchen table and began to doodle. They released from you something primal, incommunicable in any other terms, even though you could, by then, express yourself in the language of words. The drawings poured forth from somewhere in your right hand, unconnected with any other part of your physical body or your mental consciousness. It was some form of magical alchemy which had no apparent source. You were untutored in any form. Your parents did not draw and your elder brother did not draw.

Even then, I could feel the world draining out of me. The palate of my senses and sensations spreading their way across the unbound purity of those smooth, white sheets of paper.

I longed for it all day at school. Through those itching hours of reading and writing and those infuriating passages of time marked by mathematics and science. Then the ecstatic joy of the pencils, the pens, the paints, the clay, and that magnetised artificial world that seemed to me to encompass life itself: art.

'This drawing shit's a waste of time. My old man reckons they'd be better trying to teach us something useful, like mending cars.'

'It's all those posh arty cunts making us do it.'

'I wish they'd give us more PE instead.'

'It's alright for you. You can draw things properly.'

'You're teacher's little pet, aren't you?'

'I think he wants to bum you. Spread them wide and stick it in hard.'

'If we paid you, you could do our drawings for us. Then we'd all pass and they'd all look good.'

They carried him there upon a worn old stretcher under the full glare of a midday sun. He lay on the stench-ridden canvas soiled with a cancerous sweat. He wheezed and coughed until his chest ached with pain and he screamed in despair. They carried him here to this place where the women would tend him. It is to be his cenotaph.

The dark is circling in. It covers everything: my eyesight; my hearing; my sense of smell; my hands; my feet; my external focus. It is cramming into me, all of my inner space, all of my inner organs and all of my inner functions.

The wide excrement stain is pasted hard now against the cotton sheet. Every now and then, the stain expands and darkens further. His consciousness is no longer aware of his expulsions.

Death is an infuriating rage against our physical beings. It cannot be tamed or suppressed. It carves each monstrous slither of flesh until it has been sated with its full pound. It is the indomitable will of nature to turn all that was once life into rotting vegetation: mere fertiliser for the dusty, baked earth.

She lay still on the bed, didn't she? The images of the world no longer projected into her through the retinas. There was a small plastic bottle that the inquest would term barbiturates. You picked them up and spoke their correct pharmaceutical name into the telephone as you called for an ambulance. You can't remember the word now. It all felt so ghostly unreal then.

'Is her chest moving? Is she breathing at all? Do her eyes show any sign of life? How long has she been alone in the flat? Are those prescription drugs that she normally takes? Were they prescribed for her by her doctor? How long has she been taking that prescription? Has she tried anything like this before?'

Later, you pondered if it all really happened. She went through this, which you feel now, back then, so long ago. Her arm was cold: frozen. Not a glimmer of anything. And you loved her; not then, but before. The duvet lay across her. You remember purchasing it together. Her mother's eyes stared past you, out into a vision of a grave which would greet her daughter, even though it would be a cremation: smoke stacks in the sky.

Then we are one with the ether once more.

I had loved you; not then, it's true. I told you I loved you still: I lied. I never thought you would do it. I couldn't imagine such a thing. Twenty-four years of age, you were. It wasn't long enough for you to have recognised the world. Your place in it. Your possibilities. You never knew yourself. I couldn't fathom you, either. You wanted me to explain it to you. I couldn't then. I couldn't now. Perhaps you were right. It's all erased in the end. Our greatness, our smallness, our weaknesses, our virtues and our sins. They flush out into the cosmos, never to return. We are forgotten before we are given time to remember ourselves. The wretchedness you must have felt. You were dead already by the time I had returned. It was all over: for eternity. There was no use in loving you then. It could never be reciprocated again. They were dead feelings. As dead as your eyes.

The creatures of the night come out and ravage about. With tenacious paws they struggle against the harshness of the desertscape. The nocturnal world has a different edge to it. It is mysterious and enigmatic, ferocious and cunning. The sounds whisper out from the darkness, speaking of adventures and calamity, and ultimately death. Always that stench pervading over all. Carried across the parched land upon those hot, sandy winds. The herdsmen all sleep tightly out in the wilderness. They will protect their livestock to their last defiant breath. To do so is to protect life itself.

My god, how the body clings on. Hoping, even now, for further life. Emaciated beyond all recognition. When does the heart choose to stop beating? Is this still a man? Can a human being exist beyond this endurance? Where is the mind?

It was withering on the vine by the teenage years. But the art teachers knew you were a star in ascendance. When two of your friends were suspended from school for a fireworks stunt in a corridor, you escaped the headmaster's wrath with a week of lunchtime detention. Where are they now? The two friends you so righteously abandoned. It was the art department which rescued you and afterwards, in your penitent state, it was they who resuscitated you.

'You have something the others don't have: talent. You need to use it or lose it,' the head of the art department declared.

'We see so many kids come through here; some are destined for a better life than their parents, a lot can expect the same. Most of them are just biding their time before being set loose on the world. So we do what we can to prepare them for the shock of it all. But you; you have a great opportunity to have a different kind of life. With your talents, who knows? You could go all the way and make a living as an artist, which isn't an easy thing to do, you know, believe me. You could even become rich and famous; it's been done. But the matter is, it's a terrible shame to waste a wonderful opportunity like yours. An opportunity that doesn't come around every day.'

He lies still in a stale, atrophied state: malarial in its ferocity. The sweat lines splay out a marooned apparition on the soiled sheets. The shroud of a corpse incarnate and physically impaled upon the terse cotton weave. A salt-inhaled mask of death ready for the purifying fires of the funeral pyre. The thin mattress, infected by his disease-ridden carcass, will also be dowsed in those purging flames.

In the morning the local elders must surely meet to discuss what is to be done with this fever-ridden stranger in their midst. A man from foreign lands, who has travelled great distances, at such a cost.

On a washing green, in the dry warmth of an early May day, playing two-touch football with a pal, you took a hat from a stranger and placed it on your head. You gave scant regard to the colouring, nor the lettering. It held the sun at bay from your eyes as you drank headily of childhood freedom, so far from the endeavours of the adults' world.

When you went home for your evening meal your father tore the hat from your head in anger and despair.

'What are you doing with that thing on your head? Where did you get it from?' my father asks harshly.

'I don't know, some woman,' I reply sheepishly.

'What woman? Give me that bloody thing here,' he fumes.

He placed it in the sink, poured lighter fluid over it and set it on fire. In disbelief, you witnessed the cleansing flames purify a malignancy of thought and a piece of the innocence of childhood. Then your father sat gloomily in a chair in the kitchen, smoking a cigarette and tugging back tentatively on a solitary can of beer before staring off into some unseen and unknowable political abyss.

The unseen heat stalks the room, colonising every conceivable crack of space. His wheezes rattle through the oxygenless air. The night no longer cries, a howling madness grips his soul.

Can it now be so near? The moment of reckoning? A life in the womb vacated so as to stumble towards the tomb. A register of momentary recollections of abbreviated experiences, carried to this precise locale to be discarded into biological disintegration.

A black cat lying prostrate against the little bitumen-treated wooden fence. Solidified against the cold, damp morning air. Its dark, blood-dappled right eye loosened in its socket: its left eye missing. The front right leg snapped like a twig in the wind. Death held dominion over that dark and bluff February morning. A poor animal, a family pet, run over and discarded by the side of the road. Its corpse had been cleared away by home time.

'The poor thing,' my mother consoles impotently.

The council men had worked fast. By nightfall the cat was rotting in the local rubbish tip, a stinking carcass with a blue collar dangling loosely around its broken neck.

Aged seven, it was my first glimpse of death. It was a strange and sickly, wandering kind of feeling I had all day. A sadness I carried with me, as I stood distanced from my classmates. An emotion I could not fathom, nor articulate. I had no words for it. Instead, I drew a picture of a wood, with a winding path, the trees bent over in a foreboding huddle, as though whispering their enticements to follow along their gloomy tunnel. At the end was a dark figure, half-turned towards the viewer. The pencil markings were deep and dark, etched hard into the rough, grey paper. The teacher examined the work then put it aside and said nothing. In truth, what was there to say?

You understood this composition better when you first witnessed a print of Dürer's: *Ritter, Tod und Teufel*. It took you immediately back to that strange picture of death and mortality which you created as a child. You realised then it was not solace in the dead cat you sought, but in your own terminal condition. The fear and melancholy were powerful sedatives as an adult staring at that solipsistic Teutonic hero, indignant of his fate or destiny. If you could only have drawn anything half as well. You turned on your desolate heels and vacated the museum.

I feel nothing of that Germanic hero's strength as I lie facing the abyss. I am neither ignorant nor indifferent to that shadowy figure possessed of an hour glass. The landscape so different from here, where hollow, sand- and wind-blasted skulls pepper the way into the badlands of the desert. My wish is only for that knight's courage and for Dürer's faith, and yet I have neither.

Did I ever possess such a thing as courage? Edgy and aware from the beginning, carving my way along all the shadows of the walls, I attempted to navigate my existence through the cracks in the social jungle. I contrived my faith to be carefully composed in the self.

I felt safe in the margins, with the creatures of the nocturne. Those of us who crept stealthily through the dark passages of the heavy summer holidays, even though they were well lit, with bright sunshine.

I took trepid footsteps into the world of sports and competitive masculinity. Never finding a home for myself there. Yet they had to be navigated: my father and brother accepted no less. My mother fretted morosely from the sidelines. She was incapable of intruding, for fear of stigmatising and stymieing me further.

'Well, if he hit you, hit him back twice as hard,' my father would scold.

'Your brother will teach you. You teach him to defend himself.'

My brother stepped into the ring only too willingly. 'Right then, you wee tit, put up your mitts and prepare to be slaughtered,' he goaded gleefully, before raining down the blows fully upon me, harder than any kid on the street would have done.

On the warm concrete paving stones you amused the others with your draughtsmanship, complete with adventurous and comical commentaries. Sometimes, the rain would wash them all away. Sometimes the teenagers would come in the evening, intoxicated with strong lager and cider, spitting long gobs of phlegm into your characters' faces then rubbing their spit in with their aggressively laced-up boots.

'What's all this shit, then?'

'Enough of your baby drawings, go and fuck off, it's our space now.'

'Did you draw this, wee man? It's quite funny.'

There were still the cartoons showing in the mornings. You watched them with a feverish intensity. Sitting cross-legged on the floor with the swirling acid-coloured pattern of the carpet floating around your periphery. The curtains were held firmly closed to protect you from daylight as you ate your crispy bacon sandwich with lashings of ketchup and glugged at your concentrated orange juice. When you laughed, pieces of sandwich fell from your mouth and you greedily scooped them back in again. You watched anything they showed: *Tom and Jerry*, *Donald Duck*, *Mickey Mouse*, *Pluto*, *Goofy*, *Sylvester the Cat and Tweety Pie*, *Pepé Le Pew*, *Bugs Bunny*, *Daffy Duck*, *Speedy Gonzales*, *Wile E. Coyote and the Road Runner*, *Yogi Bear*, *Wacky Races*, *Spiderman*, and your favourite - *Scooby Doo*.

Under the covers on those warm, halcyon nights, you switched on your little soldier's torch and surreptitiously read your comics: *Batman*, *Superman*, *Spiderman*, *The Beano*, *The Dandy*, *Commando*, *Asterix*, *Tintin*, *Oor Wullie*, *The Broons*, and the ubiquitous *Mystery Gang*.

He always hated comics and cartoons, my brother. My father could not see much worth in them, either. My brother read football books and sporting annuals. He watched *Grandstand* and *World of Sport*. Dreamed of being Eddy Merckx or Johan Cruyff. Whereas I would have chosen Chuck Jones.

'Fuckin' waste of time, those cartoons. What a load of pish,' my brother declares.

'You in there, stop swearing and just let him watch his shows. He always lets you watch yours,' my mother shouts in from the kitchen.

'I'm just waiting for the snooker to come on,' he whines.

'So wait,' she declares.

'You're fuckin' dead,' my brother snarls at me in vengeance.

The sad, disquieting hush of the night tugs at the fringes of the distant blackness. The stars are endless in their moribund prominence across the screed of dark horizons. The scenery is monochromatic, as the moon cannot spare enough luminance to light up the ochre in the light soil. The morning sun shall be blessed with a range of colours in the stratosphere.

He gasps and clamours for air to fill those liquid lungs. A murmuring groaning comes from inside the throat, a rattle against the stagnant heat of a heaving continent pressed hard against the crumbling walls.

For a period in your adolescence, the obsession of trying to capture the bed sheets took root. Each and every day you began again with the folds, the shadows and the textures you had viewed in Da Vinci's work. You worked in graphite, charcoal, chalks, pen, ink, and even paint. You felt that to master the nature of materials was to conquer form. Mornings and nights studying creases, outlines, shapes and ridges. Like sketches of great mountain ranges: the Alps, the Andes, the Sierras, the Rockies, the Himalayas. Your mother felt you strange, your father felt you pointless, your brother called you 'prick'.

When older, you marvelled at the Greek sculptures in the British Museum, their clothing carved immaculately, their craftsmanship beyond comprehension and so superior to the Roman dilettantes who came later. You touched those garments, wishing the genius of those artists to pass through the ages on to you.

My skills with a pencil developed into a social skill, also. Drawing all over their canvas bags for them. Celtic crosses were in and I drew that one on the arm of that boy and he used it as a marker for a homemade tattoo. The police came to the door, because he blamed me.

'He says it was you, son, plain and simple.' The police officer sits, smugly fixing me with his condescending stare. Waiting patiently for his cup of tea from my mother.

'There's no possible way he could have done that to himself. He needed accomplices. And, quite frankly, he named you.' The pig bastard glances over to my father and shakes his head. My brother mimics him, smiling grimly underneath.

'He's a good kid really,' my father meekly opines.

'That's how they all start out. Every one of them. Trust me, they're all good kids,' comes the cynical riposte. My brother is once more nodding like an eejit.

I was eventually beaten for it. Slapped in the face for lying and saying it wasn't me that inked the tattoo. My father was terrified I would go to borstal. I was always cold towards him after that. Never could forgive him, even though he hadn't done it before and nor did he do it again. Fourteen or fifteen years old. Too old for a beating, I thought. Not like my mother smacking us when we were younger. He split my lip. Offered me his handkerchief afterwards. I said no. I just let the blood sit in my mouth as I fumed in my room and wished them all dead.

Outside, in the vast wilderness, the sand sits stagnant and haunted. The witching hour has descended, as the moon passes shadows over the hot, deflated lands. Those little grains of unformed glass baking beneath the soles of the feet.

Standing on that wide expanse, staring out into the unfathomable green-and-blue of the North Sea. The waves skimming along the edges of the beach. Watching the older boys constructing a floating craft, an orphaned raft, through the use of empty metal barrels and orange rope. They had lashed this ship of fools together with supreme concentration and consternation. Working energetically as an anarchic team of demotic engineers. They built the errant vessel quickly as it was the last days of the summer holiday. They asked this silent watcher by the shore if he wanted to play a role in the construction but the answer was no, due to the lack of any aquatic ability, coupled with the mortality fixation of drowning.

'Do you want to give us a hand, pal?' one of the boys asks enthusiastically.

'You can come out to sea with us in it afterwards if you want. There's plenty of room for everyone,' another offers kindly.

29

'No, I'm alright,' I answer with a quiet embarrassment.

How I loved the water, and yet never learned to swim. They couldn't teach me, any of them. The teachers; the friends; my mother and father; my brother through his means of tough love by trying to drown me. I refused all remonstrations. To me it was enough to capture the water's allure in paints. To marvel at the dexterity and determination of Turner. To be master of the sea and not allow it to triumph and ultimately realise that one can never be master of the sea, or nature itself.

The ships drowning upon the rocks and I never made it. The trip down the Rhine gorge passing by Lorelei. I was holed up drunk in a little provincial Teutonic hotel, run by the old oompah bandman with his walrus moustache. As though some antiquated throwback to the time of the First World War. We both laughed at him behind his back and called him Der Kaiser. His guttural and gruff German belied a kind and gentle soul, prone to bouts of gregarious laughter. At what his humour was aimed we could not tell, as he spoke so little English and we so little German.

Into the blackness of the night. The darkest night on earth. A quelling hush which will last an eternity. And the herdsmen will slumber on in to the newly dawning light. Rising up across the vastness of the desert sands, across thousands of miles, from the warm, translucent currents of the Indian Ocean.

He will sleep, still. He will never end with his sleep. The sleep of the dead. The infiniteness of a breathless unconsciousness. The coming dawn will rob him of all memory and all time. Before him, the blank canvas of a volumeless space. A space which can never be filled.

Down through Provence with its lavender fields and the great Mont Sainte-Victoire, so recognisable from all those Cezannes. The Côte d'Azur all touristy and flatulent. With all of its *poseurs* and *flâneurs* on the quaysides and La

Croisette, and a million over-bloated yachts. But the blue of that sky washed clean by the mistral. The bluest blue ever. An endless Klein up in the heavens.

You walked into the chapel at Saint-Paul de Vence and looked at those drawings. The stations of the cross rendered so beautifully, as never before. Even that great draughtsman himself, Picasso, was jealous: condemning Matisse as a hypocrite and unbeliever.

The robed priest resplendent in the coloured light. You traced those marks with your eyes. How clean and clear those lines were. Everything superfluous removed; erased by a master. An ulterior reality transposed upon those tiles. The image of a man, not in God's image, but in man's image. The expression of an individual: an avatar for all priests. Just lines and marks and stains on a wall, like the first cave paintings.

What is in the human heart and mind? How can we render such a thing as it truly appears to us? In our consciousness and our unconsciousness, our dreams and fables, our realities and torments, our heavens and hells.

You wanted to draw it, to draw all those things. You wanted to create another reality: another earth. You failed. In your wildest imaginings, you failed. You failed to conceive of another reality which could be superimposed upon this one. It was not possible. The world surrounding us can only be eradicated through death. There is no cure. Art is a failed project, because human beings are failed projects. Human beings are flawed beings and all the gods in the universe can't change that. But you could not be content with a failed attempt, you drew on regardless.

'We must slay our fathers; topple our gods,' I declared to the world. A youthful manifesto to future posterity.

The sweats and coughing. Those strange dreams conjured up amidst the utter blackness of the night. Living as a derelict in that old vicarage near Southwell. Sparsely furnished. A restoration project a gallerist allowed you to live in, survive in, for a few months as you got well. The sickness and weariness from a wayward existence. The success mired in alcohol and drugs, your veins filthy with extruded poisons. You lay on the mattress on the floor, despairing, clutching the woollen blanket around you. It became your comforter, like the one you had as a child. You cried for every bitter moment you had tasted in life.

Your hands couldn't work anymore. Your brain was a damp mass of electrical activity passing through it on the way to nowhere. Your stomach retching from moment to moment. The cold sweat inching over every strip of your anatomy. So repulsed by yourself and so desperately wanting to be accepted. No longer the rebellious flame in the pit of your stomach. Now, just a wide-reaching disgust with everything.

When the news came through on the telephone of you being lost at sea with your six shipmates, in a winter storm south of the Shetland Islands, I couldn't rationalise it.

We were one. We were brothers and yet we were separate: had always been separate. We neither liked nor loved one another. We had barely spoken over the preceding ten years.

'Son, it's your brother. I've got terrible news. I'm sorry. I'm so sorry. But he's lost at sea, presumed dead,' my mother tells me in a half-trance.

Her voice disbelieving, monotonous, somewhere far out past those raging currents which dragged your vessel and all its crew down into the murky depths of the North Sea.

I couldn't say anything. I had no words with which to communicate. I said I would return home immediately.

I went straight to the studio. Circled around it vaguely for some time before sitting down at the large wooden desk in the centre of the space. I took a big sheet of crisp white paper and marked a circle in the centre. I began to fill it with tight graphite marks, followed by charcoal, then black ink, finishing the composition off with black oil paint. I worked ferociously without rest for five hours solid. Exhausted, I finally set down the brush and lifted the paper above the plane of the table. The centre sank with its weight, its dark mass pulled by gravity ever further down.

You walked into the nearest pub. The one you occasionally used for a quick lunch or for an interview with a journalist. You drank twelve-year-old malt whisky. You drank ten. Then you staggered home drunk and emotional. You fell into your bed and you wept for your drowned brother. You did not rise for three days. You glugged water and did not eat. You did not wash. You did not answer the phone. You never returned home. You never returned home again.

He lies there parched, his tongue unable to capture any moisture. The sweat secretions in his anatomy have all run dry. There is only a hopeless panting in the scorched darkness of the night. The bodily structure weakened beyond repair. A corpse in the process of burying itself before its residual demise.

The land breathes stagnantly across the dark desert plains. Its dry and calcifying breeze splaying the hot, rigid sands into new forms of winding dunes. The herdsmen sleep on. What dreams awaken them? The same visions that torment other men? Do they simply carry within them images of the lands they wander and the homes to which they will return?

They built a cairn for them. A memorial facing out to sea. The crew's names all etched upon it. My mother sent a photograph to me with its image emblazoned upon it. I held it for a few moments then hid it among some other things and never bore witness to it again. His death an absurdity, another abstraction of reality. Never clear in my mind why he hated me so. Should I have grieved more for him? Would he have grieved for me in return?

In spite of the dark, the heat burns on. Entering through the small slip of a window and clasping at the thick walls. Radiating viscously through the putrid, thin air. The lungs cannot amass enough oxygen to breathe fully. The heat sucks all life from the room. Not even the cockroaches survive.

Lying out on a tartan blanket on the lawn in the July sunshine, in your friend's expansive garden. His house with its gravel drive so different to your own small social-housing hutch. His parents were a dentist and a solicitor: they worked all the time. You didn't know why he had you around the place. You considered only that you must have amused him. He referred to you as 'The Communist', due to your vague political orientation. He teased you about it, but viewed in your eyes a righteous passion. A belief his indolent nonchalance could not redeem. He had a smooth all-round tan from a previous fortnight in the Algarve. He was handsome and toned, never without a girl; and they were always of the best. They tolerated you with a bemused detachment. You were the holy fool. The boy who could draw anything. You drew every one of them, the whole crowd, and astounded them all with your talent and skill. They laughed at the big black-framed glasses you wore when you sketched and they gawped fervently at the images you produced. They were mindfully detached from their portraits but always returned home with them.

It was his sister, two years older than us, who captured my attention. Her long red hair - his was blond - she took from her mother. She would glance hello in passing then fold back into her mysteriously gilded world. She once asked if I drew the picture pasted by way of magnets onto the fridge door. A quick throwaway sketch of the garden that her father had taken a notion for.

'That picture, there, on the fridge; did you draw it?' she inquires coyly, her bare foot against the cupboard, a cold bottle of mineral water in her hand.

I respond with a simple 'Yes'. To which she flits away without comment.

They were never solicitous with one another. Always well-mannered and coolly indifferent. No hysterics in the family, no animosity. It was all ghostly unreal for me, so unlike all the other households of my friends. They lived in some frigid frontier where emotions were relegated to superfluity.

He tossed you one of his former belles to play with: gave his assent to the whole charade. She circled around you for a while, amusing herself.

'What are you sketching now, Marx?' she teased.

Breezy, ferocious, witty, pretty, and sexually precocious. At sixteen years of age she was already adept at pulling the wings off the boys. You were lost, completely adrift and beyond your wildest capabilities. She gave you peer cache you couldn't possibly have hoped to emulate. For six and a half weeks she took your hand, dated you, hustled for you, and then kissed you off with a blowjob in her bohemian-chic bedroom.

I was relieved to capitulate to the end of the farce. She was never mine. I could never have belonged to her. She died of breast cancer aged thirty-two. She was married to a successful building contractor, with one child. I only found out years later. Long after her body had decomposed. I kept two drawings I made of her. She kept only one sketch of many. A sad, melancholic pose that she said made her look somewhat innocent. She seems a strange and exotic caged bird now in my memory. How many times did I give over a thought to her throughout the years?

A pale amber glow creeps surreptitiously across the wall and onto the ceiling, as two low voices pass under the window of the baked heaving mass of his room. The language remains as foreign to him as when he first heard it. He can, though, discern that they are female voices which trail off into the dark hum of the night.

Perhaps mother and daughter, or sisters on an errand of mercy. Does the dawn approach? Am I to witness yet one more day on this red, cracked bitch of an earth? Shall I hear the song of one more morning bird or the grunting and hissing of a feasting vulture?

Wearily, his predeceased body rolls painfully over, towards the source of light and voice, but they have already disappeared into the vast expanse of the desert blackness which surrounds everything in this remote part of the cosmos.

We climbed up in the darkness to greet the worn old Château of La Coste. There we sat amongst the endless stars and the drumming July heat; a cloudless, windless night with no mistral in sight. The building was in murderous ruin: its patron saint long since commanding his repose in hell. We giggled through acid-rimmed teeth, all seven of us. The concoction of pointlessly rambling horror stories, invented in permanently disintegrating minds, filtered into the beating Provençal air.

'When they finally liberated the castle, during the revolution, they found hundreds of corpses from the surrounding villages, but nobody from this one. The villagers here helped kidnap people from the other villages for the Marquis to violate and murder, but he was unfortunately holed up in the Bastille at the time.

'The revolutionary troops from Marseille, which liberated La Coste, found heads on poles, innards strung up like Christmas lights, severed arses hanging off the battlements in humorous defiance against the liberators. They discovered a dozen fires filled with the bones of the murdered and the air stank with the acrid stench of burnt human fat.

'They made thick broths and *boudin noir* with the victim's blood.

'Tough, seasoned and patriotic soldiers fell to their knees and wept at the sight. In vengeance, they rounded up all of the adults in the village; those who hadn't yet escaped into the countryside, and severed their limbs, then hanged their still-twitching torsos from the trees. They tied people up, together in a tight group, with rope, and then blasted grapeshot out of a cannon at them. Those poor, young revolutionary guards, my god but they couldn't kill those wicked and evil wretches fast enough.'

This was one wag's salaciously gruesome reportage. A tale which held us all revoltingly enthralled.

The muted colours of the night, the village, and the valley below swarmed around our recalibrated minds. Bottled water was passed around as arsenic poison. Smoke rings from greedily ingested joints filled with Lebanese hashish. A couple sneaked off to fuck under the dark silhouette of the ominously brooding ruins. I drank a litre of red wine and pissed much of it up against the castle walls, before stumbling through the quietly dense village streets and slumping sleepily into the back of the car which had brought me there from Marseilles.

A wind ascends out in the scrubbed dunes. It dusts sand up into the airless night and through the window of his room. Some grains fall stagnant on the withered, disease-ridden sheets. Small movements in his corpse cause them to chafe roughly against the dank moisture weeping into in the hard cotton weave.

It first happened when you were thirteen. Your brother was out celebrating a football win with some pals. You sneaked over to his bed and fed your hand underneath his mattress. There you retrieved the items you knew he stashed there. He was sneaky enough to fool your mother, but not clever enough to contain the subterfuge from your spying eyes.

You took the magazines into bed with you and in the darkened hush of the room you proceeded to view their prurient charms with a torch under the covers. A young, nubile blonde in a barn, romping around in the hayloft in various poses of disarm. A brunette draped her naked flesh from pillar to post in a macho, leather-and-chrome penthouse suite.

They was plenty enough mischief to arouse you and reimagine for the express purpose of masturbation. Which you embarked upon, just in the way all the other boys described it. Then it happened; the strangest, most shocking, and most wonderful sensation of all your young life, and suddenly it was out there in the world: *Ecce Vita*.

'Fuck, that was nice,' I whispered into the darkness.

I had corrupted myself. At church they said it was wrong: morally wrong. At school, they told us it was a natural act. A progression towards adulthood. It wouldn't have mattered either way; there was nothing that was going to stop me from committing that act again and again and again, sinning on throughout my entire life.

It progressed from the ecstatic into the banal. I wiped the viscous, cloudy fluid from the magazine page onto the cotton sheet. The air beneath the blanket was filled with a pungent, earthy smell I had never encountered before in my life. By equal measure alluring and repulsive. A smell I would later identify as the stench of life.

You grew adept at reproducing those images of women from magazines for the other boys, drawing them time and time again, for your own amusement as well as theirs. Finally, you began to reproduce them for payment by readily eager teenagers, who would then hide the obscene images inside schoolbooks and underneath loosened floorboards in their bedrooms. You spent all of your ill-gotten gains purchasing records by the likes of The Velvet Underground, Lou Reed, Iggy Pop, The Sex Pistols, The Clash, The Skids, The Buzzcocks, The Jam, Blondie and Joy Division.

You had no other means of income. Your parents had little money to spare and though your brother worked on building sites he refused to pass on a penny, for lack of sibling empathy.

In the dust-baked plains he resides, edging ever onwards into the tomb. The recesses of the memories dulled but still illuminating. Is it when the memories end that the man does too? Is this the place we may term death in the soul? Why is the world we inhabit so different to that of our dreams?

Why did she kill herself?

The grief took years before it began to torment you. Passing through New Street station, you were reminded of her. The semi-detached house in Solihull where you spent a Christmas with her family; the mother, the father and the older sister. They never saved her, either. Her ups and downs, highs and lows, kept on coming in waves, until it was all so impossible to cope with.

'When are you two lovebirds going to tie the knot, then? Such a scandal living in sin like that,' her sister laughs mockingly.

'We're bohemians,' I counter, 'and there are no marriages allowed in Bohemia.'

'Bullshit, you're common garden variety bourgeois,' her sister dismisses me.

I look at the sister, impressed by her contemptuous demeanour and wonder if I wouldn't mind fucking her, too.

Was I truly so callous? An exhibition to organise. What show was it? I have no knowledge of the event now, or how successful it was.

The game must be played out to the end. That's what you told yourself. Be a professional at all costs. She was dead and that was that. She was dead and you had survived.

His heart creaks on, slowly garrotted in its own rib-formed hell. The lungs gently oozing out of their cage. The body disintegrating: the soul carousing on towards oblivion.

The hot dust and sand scatter listlessly across the floor of the room, just as these particles do outside in the plains and dunes. Out there in the night, the herdsmen sleep, the cattle sleep, and in here soon so shall he. The darkness of eternity forever closes in.

Shaded in a luminous light, you walked along the summer street with the news in your heart. You had fooled them: fooled them all. They had accepted you for art school. It hadn't seemed likely they would. It was impossible that you could have dreamed such a thing. No one had ever been before. Not one member of your family had ever made it into the corridors of a university.

No longer an art star, now just another upstart. There were hundreds of stars. Hundreds of teacher's pets. They were ten-a-penny. Better educated than you. Better travelled, and better bred. A miserable little fucking parvenu from the provinces. If you worked hard, you could get yourself a teaching post in the art department of a modern secondary comprehensive. Get a semi with a little garage attached, to paint in during your long holidays. Art school was the world of the cool and hip and you were neither. You did what you always did in such circumstances: you faked it. You tried out several personalities in the course of four years. In the end, through sheer force of will, you blossomed into you.

I felt odd at first: detached. Working in that white cubed space with her. The girl the boys all loved. Her ironic black-on-white striped dress, her black leggings and black ballet pumps. Her bobbed, bleach-blonde hair with the black French beret on top and the black leather bomber jacket. Her pale skin and her bright red lipstick. I looked like a farm labourer in comparison. Then I tried on everyone else's style. I knew she could never be mine. She was the source of all my fantasies and more than a few of the others' also. Her boyfriend was that sporty architecture student two years older, who had once acted in a film.

But she couldn't draw like you. Then the others soon found out that they couldn't, either. She would take friends round, to your shared space, to show them your work. She was proud of you. She was supportive of you.

'Look at how fucking brilliant he is. Nobody can draw like

him. He's the Rembrandt of the school. This little place couldn't cage him. He's going to be a monster hit in the art world once he leaves here,' she proclaims victoriously to her gathered cohort of acolytes.

She became your friend and champion. And when you went home, in the dark space of your bedroom, with your eyes clenched tight, she became your girlfriend and fucked you.

You drew her face once, in monochrome, with the only colour the red for the lips. She stared at it for a long time. You nonchalantly told her she could keep it. She quietly removed it from the board, rolled it up and left, without another word.

I was eventually glad to be rid of her. She moved on to lens-based media in the second year. Making 16mm films starring herself. I don't remember them now. I could finally work in peace, without distraction, my new cubicle partner being a male and a total asshole. I felt at home sharing a space with someone with whom there was a puerile, mutual antagonism.

'I would have used a touch of red in with the black to make it darker,' he says, pointing to a spot on a still-wet painting.

'It looks kind of derivative of Soutine, but without his passionate angst.' Typical of his modus operandi. Name an artist to show off your knowledge of art history, then give some trite pseudo-intellectual commentary afterwards.

'It's just Warhol, but without the insouciant wit,' he tells me, staring at a self-portrait I have completed.

'Well, we can't all be geniuses like you,' I snap back, gazing upon his pastel-coloured abstract landscape, which truly resembles nothing other than a talented ten-year-old's attempt at something pastorally profound.

You travelled back and forth several times to the Scottish Museum of Modern Art to view Lichtenstein's *In the Car*. To view his clean lines, his clear vision; his cool, beguiling aesthetic. You drew all the *femmes fatales* and *ingénues* on campus. Effortlessly hip, smoking, drinking, laughing, pouting. Some posed for you: others ignored you. They could never be captured in the same way as Lichtenstein's damsels. He had discovered something: an epiphany. You were stumbling around in the dark.

The night seeps in through the window, under the walls, through the floor. It envelops everything in its blackness. Dancing around all the cracks and crevices in the dungeon-like room. It sucks all light from the world; all shapes and all forms. It blends in among itself, creating richer and darker textures. Its density growing exponentially with its destruction.

There is a form; indiscernible, incomplete. A shroud covering a barely living thing. The breath, a meek exhalation of poisoned air under cover of a sweat-stained white sheet. The folds of cotton draping downwards from a corpse with a still-beating heart.

After the longest journey I had ever embarked upon we finally reached the hallowed ground of JFK International Airport and an entire continent from the Bering Strait to Cape Horn spread out before us.

The low sun shone through the Brooklyn Bridge in a peerless late September evening and the barely ignited lights of the most dynamic place on earth bade us come and play.

You stood there on top of the world; on top of the Empire State Building. Gazing out upon the new Gomorrah, all wide avenues and phallic buildings. On that cloudy, humid morning the city was a grey landscape swept against a grey sky.

The colour was on the streets; on the sidewalks. An explosion of bustling humanity, of inchoate dynamism, of posturing and posing, of arrogance and dominance. Everyone looked glamorous. Everyone looked like a star. They were all ready for their fifteen minutes of fame, the whole damn city. We joined the throng. Imagined we were at the centre of the universe and who knows, maybe we were. In the melancholy of the plane, before taking off into a bright blue sky, I wished to stay there forever, at the centre of the maelstrom. Instead, we returned to an unseasonable snowstorm in Auld Reekie.

I took part of New York home with me. I took that colour and movement and placed it at the heart of my painting practice. I suddenly began to paint quickly and abstractly. My drawing practice took heart from the monochromatic expanse of the city's rooftops. It too entered a hyperactive, abstracted phase; all blocks of rectangular and cuboid forms. Someone lent me a book called *Delirious New York* and architecture too inspired me briefly.

By the end of the academic year, New York's influence was on the wane and my work began to recapitulate, back to a more comfortable figurative style. The faces, though, were more animated now: more expressive. I took the energy and positivity of Manhattan and put it to work on my art itself. The euphoric feeling that the Big Apple had given me was transformed into a passionate endeavour to contribute to the world. To find my place within it. That was New York's true gift. For the first time in my life I felt genuinely ambitious. I finally wanted to taste success.

His dull black eyes stare out into the darkness. Does he truly see anything anymore? Can he hear the wind casting out across the dunes? There is a mild panting in his breath. The heart lingers on, pumping the soiled blood around his limping organs. The vast expansiveness of the globe cannot penetrate those walls. The end of time. The end of space. The end of memory.

There was a photograph taken outside the Chelsea Hotel in the cracked dawn sunlight. You all smiled and laughed on your last day in the city. You held arms of warmth and love around each other. Comrades careering through the famed streets of lower Manhattan. Where is that photograph now? Who took that picture? With history held in its tender embrace. An image of youth and hope, of exploration and adventure; a photograph of living and life.

In the darkest watch of the night, the remaining embers of the fire are dead. The herdsmen sleep on, their cattle sleep on. The bright, preying eyes of wild beasts wander through the blackened land of the desert plains. Their mischief perpetually on the outer edge of the encampment. The men, experienced in the cries and calls in the wilderness, sleep with one ear constantly open to the hostility which surrounds them.

He sleeps restlessly on, murmuring his distresses and pains into an empty cell. There is nobody present to listen. He must claw helplessly against the hot, heaving walls, which move endlessly in towards his being: crushing all life from within.

When the debaucheries of your lifestyle manifested themselves so wilfully, you took flight for the first of many recoveries. A fisherman's cottage was rented for a summer season in the picturesque locale of St Ives. Filled with a radiating luminance, you conclude that the light, the warmth, the sun and the ocean would cure all the ailments of the soul.

You sat down each day on Porthgwidden Beach, glancing upon the lunar movements of the tides ebbing and flowing all day long. The green of the shallows pushing out towards the blue of the ocean deep. Squinting through sunglasses at a chaste and barren sun. At night, you lay curled in a woollen blanket before the pale orange glow of a limp wood fire. Passing each evening with the nightly vigil of the deadening flicker of an abandoned television screen. The veins all pulsing through with ill omens of a desperate rage for narcotic supplements. You drank occasional bottles of cheap, tannin-ridden reds. A sickly burning down the throat and stomach, before an insane retching took over and sent you scurrying towards the toilet pan again.

I discovered the loneliness of success to be even more burdensome than the despair rendered by mediocrity. Finding everything and everyone surrounding me playing false and inauthentic. Old friends discouraging, suspicious, envious, or contemptuous of my growing infamy. New friends and acquaintances all charmless, bullish, pretentious, or simply ruinous.

'You've changed somehow. It's funny, but I never thought you would. Perhaps some of the others, but not you,' my old cubicle partner and champion tells me when we are at the same show opening many years later. She has a small and insignificant radio show on culture. We've only been talking for five minutes.

'You're on the radio. It doesn't surprise me that you made a career for yourself in the media,' I tell her, trying to remember who she is.

'Your work hasn't really moved on from university, has it?' my other ex-studio partner comments when we meet at a party. He's now a minor art critic for a Scottish Sunday newspaper. 'It's like a pale imitation of Basquiat, but it's lacking his barometer for the zeitgeist and his work's cultural credence.'

'You're still a fucking knob, then,' I reply, leaving him standing on his own with his glass of cognac.

'You need to take the art world on and make it acknowledge how great you are.'

'You need to leave that gallery and get a better one.'

'You're too good for this show.'

'What's this self-deprecating meek and mild shit? It may play well in the provinces, but it doesn't play well with the real media here in London. Show them that you mean business. Show them some balls.'

'You acquiesce too much.'

'You're far too hostile.'

'What's with that working-class horseshit?'

'Be yourself. Be courageous. Don't be ashamed of where you come from.'

'They're all pale facsimiles of you.'
Everybody had an opinion.

The inner belief perseveringly constructed over a long, arduous period dissipates all too suddenly, revealing a brittle veneer of self-doubt followed on swiftly by self-defeat. Then those most monstrous contagions, self-loathing and self-pity, coalesce in their fullest manifestation: substance abuse.

You noticed the passing seasons for the first time while meandering through The Meadows. The kaleidoscope of colours tenuously hanging from the tree branches in autumn. In winter, the cold Arctic air brought hard frosts and a petrified silence in the white-ringed twilight. New growth abounded in the spring, giving birth to a bold and brash colouring in the park. On the warm summer afternoons, everyone in the city joined in the *tableaux vivants* at play on the scuffed, verdant grass. You sat there sketching it all, on benches, on blankets, on any seat at hand. The people, the foliage, the animals, the dampness, the scattered sunlight, the cramped places, the wide open spaces, the brooding darkness, the approaching rains, the sports, the fights, the little dramas playing out in public. You caught it all and produced a ten-foot-long frieze. Filled with posturing and joy, silence and serenity, violent storms and a murdered corpse, a dynamic composition filled with young and old, of timeless beauty and an endless melancholy.

I couldn't recall such a thing anymore. The eyesight faded to a fleeting blur. How many landscapes did I pass through? I'm robbed of the sanctum they provide. To gaze upon the earth. To feel it and to know it. What became of all these things?

The red soil sits stagnant. No wind in the air; only the hum of the brooding, ripe night. The stilting heat cracks along the walls, breaking the bones of corpses and the wills of men. All is drained dry of life within the beating beast of a distant star which burns on and burns vigorously in the blistering light of noon and the breathless silence of midnight.

It was in the third year of university that I met her. She came by the studio with a friend who was in her fourth year. She stopped and watched me work, then smiled and said, 'Hi.' It was her eyes that captured my heart first of all; so bright, so full of confidence, and so beautiful. I wonder if I blushed? She smiled wider. She told me the work was interesting. She mentioned Hogarth. I mentioned Film Noir, Sartre and The Jesus and Mary Chain. I must have blushed then: she just nodded. I told some pals and they laughed. Said I'd made a cunt of myself. A girlfriend of one knew her. She was studying History of Art. She was pretty. She was fun. She was intelligent. I had an instantaneous crush.

'You're a good artist,' she tells me, looking into my eyes, before she departs.

'Thanks,' I stumble out.

You thought it couldn't happen. You thought there was no chance of a romantic encounter between the both of you. All of a sudden you noticed her everywhere; in a bar, in a café, in the student union, in the laundrette, in a faculty building, in the street. Then she was there at a house party you and some mates weren't invited to. It didn't matter, nobody checked anyone's credentials at the door. It was the house that she shared with three other friends.

No cooling breath of air is to be found in this abode. No chill wind to press the heat out through the gaps in the walls. Just a terminal inferno which burns through a motionless desert. The land forever parched: the people forever unbroken. His throbbing temples ache silently. There is no moisture left with which to sweat and yet the pores in the skin continue to jettison their odorous secretions.

The fever can be smelled throughout the oven-sealed vacuum of the room. It is the stench of a carcass beginning to fester before it is properly deceased.

Spread out on Calton Hill in the deep spring sunshine: a blanket, a picnic, and we four. Our rations for that day on display in the centre of the tartan blanket: buffalo mozzarella, sweet tomatoes, olives, sourdough bread, and a bottle of Valpolicella poured into some plastic cups. Gazing out over the city, up towards the castle, we ate, we conversed, we harangued, we laughed, and the future laid out before us felt infinite. Later, in a pub in the Grassmarket, saturated with wine, we kissed for the first time. I thought even then of the last time we might kiss. I never could recall when that was.

'I've been looking forward to doing that,' I tell her after our first kiss.

'Well, you should have done it sooner, then.' She smiles back.

You were trapped between her beauty and charm and your desire to create an artistic legacy for yourself. Your long-held need to live your life on your own terms. Even for her, in the end, there could be no compromise. An artist must be free, you told yourself so many times in justification for your actions. Even when that dictum went against your own best interests.

Looking down the Champs Élysées, the grand axis in front of us; the Concorde, the Tuileries, the Arc de Triomphe du Carrousel and the Louvre. How many times did I traverse that street? Triumphantly, at my first small gallery show in Paris. Though the art world had moved far away from there by then. We stopped off for a greedy burger at a Quick restaurant on the Champs. Drunk on whisky and high on speed and success, we took a taxi ride around the city centre at one in the morning. The City of Lights sparkling magnificently before our eyes. Somebody mentioned that Hitler had done something similar. I declared that, unlike that monster, I was a true artist who was being fêted for their extraordinary talent and genius: for creativity, not destruction. It dampened our mood nonetheless. The booze and drugs started to wear thin: the adrenaline drained to the bone. We slumbered back to the hotel, quiet and solemn, like vampires before the dawn.

You slept twelve hours or more, greedy for the solace of your dreams. You felt disconnected to her beside you. She lay still on her side, facing the window, her shoulders gently rising and falling with her breath. The space between you and her an unbridgeable chasm. The praise and flattery singing in your ears, from the night before, now a superficial whisper in the grey afternoon light. There it had been, grimly written out on a Parisian wall by the banks of the Seine – *Espoir et Désespoir*.

'It's a wonderful show, simply marvellous.'

'*C'est formidable, Monsieur.*'

'It's the best show of the season.'

'Finally, a British artist we French can believe in and get behind.'

The next day you witnessed Degas at the Musée d'Orsay, the young ballerinas in their white tutus, translucent against the light. A paintbrush touched by God: colour; space; composition; impossible, all impossible. You were there. You stood before it. It was real. It was created by man. It was not created by you.

I left the city some days later. Does one ever leave Paris? Even now did I dream of such a place? Can it truly exist? A fairytale which has risen out of the Île de la Cité. I never wished to return. It always had too much for any one human being. Too much art: too much life.

He lies there: the last of his family. Almost a ghost himself, wrapped up in its death shroud. A movement underneath, slight and vaguely imperceptible; a moan, a groan, a failing murmur. The heat and the dark burn on.

A small boy walking along with his father. It is winter. Where were we going? A football match? To the cinema? To school? Does he take my hand, or do I take his? I cannot place it. I cannot place him. I cannot place me.

Your hand moves to draw the outline of the faces you can no longer discern. Your hand worn and arthritic. It can no longer find the means of expression, nor handle the artistic tools needed to express.

If I could only feel the snow one more time. Falling magnificently down through the universe. That cold, freezing texture that melted away in the warm embrace of my skin. To scoop up that ephemeral whiteness freshly fallen and place it in my mouth to taste its heavenly purity. To drink in its life-giving vitality without restraint. A transcendental escape from this tortured moment: from this tormented world.

The wind whips across the plains, bringing hot, stinging grains of sand through the window and scattering them through the lifeless, stifled air inside his room. The herdsmen stir briefly and cover their faces. The cattle low for a moment then settle back into their restful state. A film of dust settles upon his sheet as nature attempts its own premature burial of him.

The snow lay softly on the exterior of the bedroom window. The curtains were left ajar in the damp, orange light of the streetlamp. You and your brother stumbled around blindly with the balloons left over from Christmas and the New Year. Shooting them through an imaginary basketball hoop above the door. He played the sport at secondary school. You had never been on a basketball court and had only seen the game being played on the television and in American movies.

'You don't shoot a hoop like that. You do it like this, you fuckin' douchebag.' He fires the balloon in the air and it pops.

When the balloons had all burst you continued with the game by using an orange plastic football as a surrogate. He stared at you with such a ferocious hatred and threw the ball point-blank into your face. Your nose bled and you wiped the blood and your tears on your cold, white pillowcase. Your brother simply left the room. You told your mother it was an accident. You never discovered why he did it, nor why he detested you so.

Perched on top of the world, in a penthouse apartment on the Upper East Side of Manhattan, you survey the globe. A beautiful young woman, who was a friend of a friend, has just departed. You both drank champagne, snorted cocaine, and had sex together, several times. The downtown galleries love you. The luxury apartment has been made available to you, by an actor, who adores your work and admires your politics. He is shooting a film on location in Asia. There is a black grand piano with a discarded pizza box on top of it. There are two empty champagne bottles in the bath and half-empty flutes on a shelf. Sketches of the naked girl are scattered around the living space. You stand in your shorts, in the pale grey of the dawn, staring out across Central Park and the white blanket of snow enveloping it. You wish you were at home with your family, in a council house, eating a Christmas dinner together.

In the desert the sand buries everything: water, plants, animals, corpses, memories. There are skeletal remains here and there, uncovered by the winds, before being buried again by them. There are occasional rains, then winds, then more sand. Seasons change by variations of the heat. The nights can be cold. The sun and the winds are constants.

The heat has not lifted from his room. His fever continues to growl at the temples and drain him of whatever moisture there is left in his still-living spectral form. A bed, a sheet, a floor, four walls, a ceiling, a window, a tomb in the desert; waiting for the sands to bury it alive.

I will be gone like all the rest of them before me. Heaven or hell will not hold me captive. I will go the way of the others: the kind and the saintly; the assassins and thieves; the righteous and the damned; the malefactors and the benefactors. All the types this world cannot hold.

She came to your room. She smiled then wandered around it. She scrutinised your collection of books, neatly filed along one shelf hung on the wall above your bed: *On the Road*, *The Outsider*, *The Catcher in the Rye*, *To Kill a Mockingbird*, *An Inspector Calls*, *A Portrait of the Artist as a Young Man*, *One Day in the Life of Ivan Denisovich*, *A Kestrel for a Knave*, *Look Back in Anger*, *Saturday Night and Sunday Morning*, *A Season in Hell*, *The Flowers of Evil*, *Ways of Seeing*, *The Work of Art in the Age of Mechanical Reproduction*, *The Communist Manifesto*. She picked that book out, laughed, and inquired if you had read it. You answered vaguely that you had glanced through it. You admitted to having never read John Berger nor Walter Benjamin. Your real books were piled high on your ancient, battered hardwood desk, with the names of lots of previous occupants scrawled across it. *Da Vinci, Caravaggio, Bosch, Picasso, Matisse, The Surrealists, Dali, German Expressionism, Goya, French Impressionism, Modernism, De Stijl, Abstract Expressionism, Bacon, Freud, British Painters, Italian Renaissance, Rembrandt.*

'You like books?' She turns to me as the evening light silhouettes her slender figure and highlights the colour in her tight red dress.

'Some of them. The art ones, mostly. I prefer pictures to words. Image to text,' I reply, transfixed by you.

'I like both,' you state as you return to the works on display.

You flicked through the Caravaggio. You touched a page, tenderly, respectfully, as though the image might disappear altogether if you let your natural oils imprint upon it. Your beautiful, wide brown eyes magnetised by his splendour: his genius. Your brown, curled hair was bunched up by an orange scrunchie, revealing the soft caress of your slender neck. Your skin warm and without blemish. I wanted to kiss your neck. I wanted to kiss you all over. You turned to me as though you knew my desire and then you stayed the night.

It was *Death of the Virgin*, the details confused, in your studio space. She touched the painting, smeared red down your face. She was nude, posing in front of the picture, laughing, your breath panting, your heart racing, there was a thick brush in your left hand, dripping with black paint, you traced her outline in the now blanked-out canvas. She grasped the brush and began to paint you, the dark viscous liquid stroking you up and down, up and down.

We did once stand together under that picture, in the Louvre. You were not naked and nor was I. You spoke the fluent French that you had learned from your Algerian father. You were better travelled, more cultured, more fluid with the world than me. Your mother was an English journalist, your father an academic. He taught history and cultural studies, semiotics and philosophy. She worked for a national newspaper in London. You had a library's worth of books in your family home. We had none.

The dust-strewn plains are deserted. The large, swirling dunes are deserted. The sands sprinkle and occasionally sparkle in the deep moonlight. There is silence on the edge of the world. The silence of eternity. Of a land which has not changed since man and woman first inhabited it. Geology, geography and topography were of no use to those first dwellers. They have little use now. Time continues regardless. It cares little for the physical dimensions of nature.

He sleeps briefly, awkwardly, groaning and gnarling his teeth. He does not dream anymore. The pains will not allow such a relief. There is only reality. There is only an endless consciousness of his demise into the grave.

We learned to be together as a couple and I learned to love you. I had not loved before. You had once. You rarely spoke of him. On leaving home for different universities, he broke your heart.

We sailed down the Seine in a glass-topped tourist boat, around the tip of the Île Saint-Louis, round the Île aux Cygnes and back to Port Debilly. When I first returned without you, I retraced our journey, by boat and then on foot. Your ghost haunted the whole city. I could feel your joy everywhere. In a cheap hotel off the Boulevard Richard Lenoir, outside of a brasserie in the Place de la Bastille, in the museums and the markets, by the grave of Simone de Beauvoir and Sartre in the Cimetière du Montparnasse. I was successful. I had a show in Paris. I spent the entire time stalking the past, searching for you. Desiring nothing more than to be with you. I wonder if I ever felt so lonely again.

It was in LA that I started to take drugs. There was a party at some record company executive's home in the Malibu Colony. A beach party in February, I forgot all sense of time and place and season. A stop-off show at a trendy new LA art gallery. The gallery owner brought me out there in his red Porsche 911 Targa. Speeding along the Pacific Highway.

You snorted the cocaine because the others in the room were ingesting it. The music was loud West Coast stuff. You didn't know who the bands were. One hadn't even been signed yet. It was a demo. They were all so vital and healthy and tanned and young and confident. They spoke in pseudo-intellectual, gnomic phrases you couldn't understand.

'That's the ontological state of man and it always has been,' a man with a beard, a loose beige suit, a black t-shirt and leather loafers was proclaiming.

'It's his perpetual ability to transcend his state of being that is of value,' another similarly-attired hepcat declares.

'The world is a Kantian space; it is unknowable,' yet another chimes in.

They are pop producers, writers of television crime shows; one of the in crowd is even a sports journalist.

You wanted to be a part of it all: act effortlessly louche like them. Forget her body, static on the bed, a pupae in the cold cocoon of death. The frozen numbness of cocaine frying the senses, killing the pain and making you socially accepted, temporarily, into a new tribe. They would retreat into their sun-sparkled world and you back to London in the rain.

The air is heavy, it captures every drop of moisture in the room and leaves it hanging violently in a stagnant embrace. His lips crack open, the weakening blood-flow receding from their open sores. His right finger and thumb arthritically worrying the sheet. Gripping hold of solid matter to tether him to the physical world: the metaphysical awaits beyond the fringes of the darkness of nothingness.

Would I weep for my mother as all the others do? A skeleton in the earth alongside my father. My brother now infinitesimal faecal matter in the depths of the sea. Why should I have survived? When the others died.

Your triumph was the degree show. Making images in ink and paint on acetate and overlaying them. You created a giant collage titled *Ingénues and Parvenus: Sketches from a Dilettante*. A dense and complex six-foot wall of imagery, sketched by you over the preceding months. The female characters and male gaze intense and ambiguous. The reviews ran the gamut from proto-feminist to male-exploitative. You engendered champions and detractors from both sexes. It was the only piece people talked about.

'It's a bunch of pseudo-feminist fakery. Another straight white male usurping everyone else's position and politics for their own narcissistic agenda.'

'I think it's the best piece here.'

'It's new, it's dynamic, it's wonderful.'

'At last one of these kids can actually draw properly.'

'I don't get it. I don't see why everyone's going wild for this. I've seen lots more original and better-executed pieces scattered throughout this show.'

'It's the least worthy piece here.'

'The statement's the best part of it. The rest of it is shit.'

'He's going to have a stellar career.'

The faculty loved it, spotted a star; a student who could freely promote the art department of the university. Give their campus colleagues a bloody nose. Further individual careers in academia. She helped you. Provided you with the theory you required to accentuate the work and raise it above the quotidian. She ghost-wrote your statement for you. They thought you were talented and intellectual. It was a clever ruse. One you always thanked her for.

She lent me a copy of *The Second Sex*, which I never read. I never liked novels that much. I hadn't even read most of the books I had bought myself. Words always interested me little. I preferred the image: textural, subtle, opaque. Images spoke of feelings, emotions, the subliminal and transcendent nature of the world. They were a shortcut to our subconscious. Hardwired to appeal directly to us without the requirement of further information and critique. I had little time for the intelligentsia, academia, philosophers and critics. I preferred the cinema to the theatre; painting to poetry; television to books.

An art critic from *The Scotsman* gave you your first taste of notoriety. He was visiting the graduate show to support a niece who worked in sculpture. He reviewed you instead. Gave you a five-star rating. Called you endlessly inventive and subtly subversive. It brought you celebrity in the school, a sale, and a gallery show.

'In the stale and stultifying world of the contemporary art school, where each student is required to churn out a faded copy of the contemporaneous work awash within the international art fraternity, here stands a young man on the cusp of graduation. Who perhaps, with the right encouragement and help, may even be one of the new arbiters of what is commendable and permissible in the cultural landscape and may yet prove to be a cypher for the new world art scene, or at least one offshoot thereof,' the journalist had written.

Did we begin to end then? You took a first, as did I, but all the congratulations and the compliments and the derision went to me. You were passed over. Cast into my shadow. You never complained. You never showed envy. You remained you: iconoclastic to the end. I never did have what you had. Not the grace, nor the poise, the class or the beauty, but that stoic belief in the individual self. You never followed anyone, except you. I thought it might rub off on me, but it didn't. I discovered something else, something far more fragile, something far more tragic. I discovered fame.

It was the genesis of that so-called stellar career and you would have no need, ever, for any other. You entered into the art world, where authenticity was simply a concept, and learned how to be a *poseur*. When you first had some money you bought a second-hand Leica, because you thought it made you look more artistic. You photographed people in pubs, clubs, cafés, bars and restaurants; anywhere a sketch pad and pencil seemed cumbersome and incongruous. You grew adept at it quickly. They liked your work at the photography shop. They teased you with the moniker 'Art Star', but they showed a certain deference anyway and gave you lots of tips on film stocks and developing techniques. Momentarily, you thought of quitting drawing altogether and moving into photography as a full-time medium, and then possibly even film. It was a fleeting intuition; photography was just a tool for you, a way of possessing images quickly, which would then be transferred into the more skilful and niche medium of drawing.

The gallery put me to work quickly. They found me a studio in a converted industrial building down in Leith, where several other artists were stationed. I had to produce a second and then a third version of *Ingénues and Parvenus*. I produced separate, smaller individual works based upon elements of the original with titles such as *All the Girls are called Penelope*. These pieces were broken down further into numbered prints of the work. I sweated then froze through six months to produce them. I had a glitzy opening show in the new year, with champagne and a cheap suit. Everything sold, the gallery took thirty-five percent and I took the rest, minus various deductions. It seemed as though being an artist might prove to be a kind of a living, after all.

The plains sing their own song, washing into the desert as the earth continues to heat up further each year. The herdsmen asleep recognise this, though they are not educated men. The people understand the land, they feel it, through thousands of years of knowledge and experience, passed on from father to son, mother to daughter.

Death will know him soon and he will recognise death. Its profoundly banal and invisible face: its featureless form. It is a thing which exists and yet does not exist. Death the vacuum, which offers nothing and takes all. A moment when time is and then is not anymore.

Rainy days on Sundays, scratching around for any cartoons on the television, the ticking of the clock, attending church. Salvation from our sins. What sins? I hadn't committed any. I committed so many later. The world was so small then. Held within the confines of a few square miles. My mother and father reading Sunday newspapers. My brother playing football in the street or building in a small copse of trees by the swing park. Me at the kitchen table; drawing, as always. Making up adventures, story-boarding pictures in a jotter. The world outside an endlessly grey miasma of drizzle and downpours and cold north-east winds.

You escorted two California Rose Bowl queens home from that party in Malibu, to a two-bedroom apartment in West Hollywood. You drank some white wine while they intimated and teased about a *ménage á trois*.

One was blonde and leggy, the other brunette and rangy.

'So are you, like, going to fuck us both or what?' the blonde one trills sexily, toying with a long strand of hair.

'I want to see what you Scotchmen keep up your skirts,' the brunette lunges lasciviously.

'The term is Scotsmen and we sometimes wear kilts on ceremonious occasions,' I reply pedantically.

'Whatever,' Blondie replies.

'Isn't two beautiful women in bed a ceremonious occasion? Or does it happen to you Scotsmen every day?' Brunette goads.

Both of them looked like they could eat you alive. So flawless and fecund, like two female forms sent down from an alien planet to repopulate the earth. What man could refuse them? They sauntered off to bed, leaving you alone on a suede sofa, staring out at the lights of LA. The brunette returned presently, took your hand and guided you to her bed. You couldn't perform: the drink, the drugs, the heat, the sun, the wearying day, the jetlag, the discombobulation of life thousands of miles from home, from the real world. A strange woman: a strange bed.

'I'm sorry, I'm just so exhausted and the heat and everything. I swear this has never happened before. It's not you, though,' I stutter and stammer out.

'Don't worry about it. It's no big deal,' she says as she rolls over to sleep.

We lived together for an all-too-brief two years after university. I took a space in your flat and a place in your bed. There were four of us lodging together and sometimes more, especially at the weekends. I drew and painted and you got a job as a junior curator at a museum. It should have been an idyll, but I'm not certain it was. We always had ambition in our eyes, our careers in our hearts. I wanted to be an artist; you wanted to be a gallery owner. We both got our wishes, but not as one. Your parents encouraged and supported you; mine looked on askance. As though it was all too much, all too impossible. They found it hard to conceive that a man could make such a living as being an artist. I had to believe for everyone. It savages the soul eventually.

'You can teach now, son. There'll always be a need for teachers. Even art teachers,' my father counselled.

'You could get a job at the school back home. You can live back with us until you get yourself set up with a place of your own. It'll be a lot cheaper that way,' my mother states optimistically. 'They always liked you at that school. Knew you were talented. Stuck up for you. I'm sure they'd love to have you back. You'd be good with the kids, understand better perhaps what they're going through, because you went through it yourself not so long ago,' she added as a further incentive.

Sitting at lunchtimes by myself in a dark and dingy pub, nursing a pint and a whisky, like the other diffuse men surrounding me. The rest of the clientele were either retired or unemployed. I felt an odd affinity with them, as though we were part of the same tribe or clan; the untouchables.

There is a cry in the dark. Something feral, something animal; something human? It begins quickly, ends abruptly, and then there is silence once more. Outside in the night: a commotion. There are voices, female voices, rushing past the small opening in the wall of his room. They speak to one another in a crowded, hushed tone. The language is as impenetrable as ever. And the blackness gleams on, its journey across the land never-ending. Yet light will eventually come to resurrect the morning and give luminance to the dawn he will not witness.

I set off in the mornings with my sandwiches packed up tight in a Tupperware box. There was a kettle in the studio with a couple of permanently soiled mugs, half a dozen plastic spoons, some instant coffee, a bag of granulated sugar, and a tin of powdered milk. I sat there cold and alone, wondering if it would have been any worse in a factory, or a building site, or even a dull office with some elementary heating. A portrait of the successful young artist as a bore. I sat on an orange plastic chair and opened books on art borrowed from the national library; monographs on Renaissance artists, Baroque artists, Oriental artists, Pre-Colombian art, cave and wall art, Expressionists, Impressionists, Cubists, Pop Artists, Minimalists, photographers, video artists. I pored over image upon image. I threw blue ink over a canvas. Painted one entirely black. Drew *faux naïf* doodles. Composed a giant Mickey Mouse holding a gun to his head; one hand on his genitals while blowing his brains out. The work, the pressures, the exhaustion of the previous years, finally took their toll. I was in my early twenties and already burnt out.

You smoked cannabis in the late afternoons with a couple of the other artists, your fellow conspirators. You lied about your work ethic to her and your gallery. After the initial show there was nothing. Booze at lunchtime, dope in the afternoons, and the monotony of television at night. It became the endless cycle of your life; a life seeping away at the seams. A career already dissipating into a habitual self-questioning and burgeoning self-loathing.

'We should form ourselves into a film collective,' one dead-eyed painter proclaims.

'What kind of film collective?' a photographer asks, passing the spliff to the left.

'Pornography, of course,' the painter states before continuing. 'We can construct the sets: ancient Rome, ancient Greece, German brothels, state penitentiaries, that kind of thing. You can film and photograph them. We'll make a fortune. There's a big market for that kind of thing.' He takes a deep draw on the joint and passes it to me.

'Who's going to star in these films?' I enquire.

'Anyone,' the painter adjudicates, waving his arms in myriad directions. 'Take your pick. Everyone wants their fifteen minutes of fame, don't they?'

Might I have been anything else? A road-sweeper, a teacher, a pallet-maker, a baggage-handler, a sign-painter, an advertising executive, a wedding photographer, a dental nurse, a political canvasser, a civil servant, a shelf-stacker? Would the world be a lesser place for that?

The sands pile up upon each other, one grain displacing another, eternally, until the sun crashes into the planet and everything in history disintegrates into a matterless black hole.

I went home to visit my parents that first Christmas. I showed them a photograph of you. I was proud of you, of your beauty and your intelligence and you being so culturally sophisticated. They said you were very pretty and seemed nice. My brother stood in the kitchen with a bottle of German beer in one hand and his large-chested blonde girlfriend in the other. She was quite a catch: good looking and sexy. I envied him briefly. He joked about with me, the college boy; tried to humiliate me in his usual manner, in front of her, to double the pain inflicted.

'I'm a graduate of the university of life myself. I studied at the school of hard knocks. Not like wee pishers like you, with your cheese-and-wine parties and all your posh new mates, looking down their toffee noses at the likes of us working people,' my brother leers drunkenly at me.

He asked to see the photo of you. He showed it to his girlfriend. Said you weren't bad looking, for me. Then he used the N word and they laughed together. My father had just entered the room and before I could say or do anything to my brother in retort, my father had grabbed hold of him, cursed him for being a racist, and thrown him out of our home.

He came back from staying at his girlfriend's two days later and apologised. I was gone by then. He left for good in the spring to become a fisherman on the east coast.

You never told her, did you? That you had a racist in the family. You were so ashamed and so terrified of losing her. Your parents met her and her parents at your graduation. They were never going to have much in common. You all went to lunch together to a small Italian restaurant. Your mother anxious, out of her depth, your father stoic and polite. Her parents were magnanimous in their enthusiasm for both of you and your achievements. They came to your first gallery show; your parents didn't, your mother had the flu.

Was that the last time I saw him? Didn't we meet again after that? At a christening, or a wedding? Him on the boats, bragging to my parents about the money he was earning. He never sent any of it home. Do we get the life we deserve? Do we get the death we deserve?

I finally managed to pull it together in the autumn. I started to draw again. There I was, the lone artist in his studio, the avatar of western art; the individual genius. I composed the scenes all over the white-washed boards I had set up. Image upon image was merged, fragmented, superimposed upon one another in an endless repetition of manic creativity and despair. Placed at the heart of the maelstrom was me: composer, conductor and maestro. Surrounding me, the hallucinatory, hellish visions, of drunk and drug-fuelled imagery. A swirling, kaleidoscopic arabesque of dense detailing of the dreams and nightmares of my own mythology. One that was already collapsing under its own false promise of greatness.

In both of the three-metre-long friezes you completed, the ghostly figures of your previous exhibition were descending into their own hell, before your very eyes. Your fakeness as the great artist shone through; a charlatan hack, who had bluffed his way into the gallery, with a little guile and talent, and abused the naïve trust of his bourgeois victims. The ironic humour was enjoyed by some and disdained by others, but of course everything sold and you became famous all over again.

The sharks were circling in the chop. A collector and gallerist in London had got word about your shows and turned up at the gallery in Edinburgh for *Genius: A Personal Journey*. He quietly introduced himself, with the calm, reassuring authority of pure wealth and power. With an invisible flourish he procured the entire show, secondary works and all. He also procured you.

'This is the best work I've witnessed all year. Better than anything being produced in the Continent right now. With the correct marketing on our part and discipline on yours, we will crack the capital wide open,' the collector dispensed in a brief import of self-serving hubris, then he disappeared back into the night.

The cattle remain bedded down in the scrub, as do their protectors, sleeping always with one eye and one ear open, to the silence of the desert surrounding them. The mild rustle of a breeze; the slither of a snake over the sand; a landscape which is both subtle and deadly.

He resists it all, still; the weakening of his heart, the atrophy in his muscles, the fever in his bones. Soon, he will reside permanently in the earth, dissolving over time. Down in the pit with the rest of humanity, with the worms eating their souls.

My God, he was slick. Sharper than anyone I had ever encountered in my life. He took one look at me, one look at the work, sized it up and had it all packaged immediately, boxed and ready for its move down south to London Town. He must have spent all of thirty minutes at the show and then he was gone, trailing a vapour of indomitability; a modern-day art Caesar.

She rejoiced at it all with pride, said he was important, for you and for the future of British art. You welcomed the money, when you finally received some. It wasn't enough, though; it would never be enough. They got wealthy off you.

They always had bigger homes, bigger bank accounts, bigger offshore trusts than you. They bought and sold your labour, your talent, for ever-greater rewards. Traded it among themselves; the dealers, the collectors, the institutions. You were the silent partner, the poor cousin that got to keep the change. You resented them all from the very beginning. Your father had called them rich, immoral cheats, and that's how you always thought of them.

She gave you so much more than anyone else ever had. She bequeathed you confidence, self-assurance, determination and commitment. She made you believe in a future in which you played the central role in your own life. She instilled in you the desire to be the best you possibly could. She dragged you on demonstrations; for students, for teachers, for nurses, for the workers, for the anti-nuclear movement, for the anti-apartheid movement. She politicised you more than your father, or your class, had ever done. She showed you love and taught you sex. She cleared a path to the world for you. Then you left her.

The first time I felt the heat of the Mediterranean. A sun so fierce I hadn't imagined it possible. The cool summer rain of home transformed in a matter of hours to an intensity of light I had never experienced before. The heat had a smell all of its own. A dry, musky scent filled with dust and sweat and life itself. Everything slowed right down and shone brightly. My senses couldn't catch up with it all. Then, of course, that language, everywhere: nonsensical, abstract, exotic, impenetrable. A palm tree; a real, living, breathing palm tree. An image from James Bond. Cars driving madly on the wrong side of the road, drivers tooting, honking, gesticulating in ways I couldn't comprehend. The land of the ancients: of trade and commerce and wars and conquests and religion and oppression and slavery and barbarity and food and drink and history and politics and science and philosophy and literature and culture and art. The genesis of western civilisation.

That first trip abroad opened your eyes, as though for the first time, to a world you had never encountered, except through the third-party medium of television and cinema. You realised then that the planet was a large and diverse place, filled with opportunities and possibilities. Your dilapidated studio in Leith suddenly appeared moribund, so you swapped it for something similar in the East End of London.

She could have left with me. She ended up passing through London anyway, on her career trajectory through New York, San Francisco and Paris, before returning to Edinburgh again. I never asked and she never offered. We discussed it briefly years later, when our paths crossed at an art fair.

'I thought I would stop moving in Edinburgh. That everything would slow down and my career would stall. It all seemed, somehow, too easy, I suppose,' I offer limply.

'Well your career's certainly taken off now. I'm really pleased for you. I mean that,' she counters warmly.

She thought I didn't want her to move with me and I thought her career was far too important for her to consider giving up her position at the museum. We were both wrong, or perhaps both right.

You thought it would be easy, that everything would fall effortlessly into place. You didn't truly know what an *enfant terrible* was until you relocated down south. London was heaving with them. They took up space everywhere: in artist studios and galleries, in recording studios and on film sets, in theatres and in restaurants. Every bad boy/bad girl, celebrity-hungry, fame-seeking wannabe on the planet appeared to have gravitated to London. It made Edinburgh feel like a little village; comfortable, safe and secure in its petit bourgeois tastes. At least that's what you conditioned yourself to believe. You chose to ignore the fact that London visited Edinburgh for a few weeks every August to test out their latest *succés de scandale*.

It wasn't glamorous, at least not back then, the East End. It was still the East End. You were harassed, manhandled, beaten several times - for no apparent reason - and mugged twice; once for a cheap digital watch, the second time for £7.50. You sustained, on separate occasions, a black eye, a bloody nose, several bruised ribs, bleeding from your right ear, and once had the threat of a Chelsea smile performed on you at the hands of a fifteen-year-old wielding an orange Stanley knife. He cut your jeans and superficially slit your inside thigh instead.

'What you lookin' at, you gay cunt? You fuckin' want some? You want fuckin' stripin' up, then. Let's have some, you fuckin' poncy wanker.' He snarls mercilessly at me as he moves menacingly closer.

They shrugged at A&E and they shrugged at the local police station. You very quickly learned to mind your own business and travel cautiously, especially after dark.

You remembered those kicks and barbs and stings, like a wounded and beaten dog, when convalescing years later. Along with your father's slap, a punch in the stomach received one time after school aged eight, and some kid who boxed your ears with both fists in the same instant so you couldn't hear properly for several days. The same indignities and humiliations that always returned to haunt you in your most desperate and lonely moments. You heard them and saw them, witnessed them all again, as you walked along the beach or through the countryside, cleansing body and soul, recalibrating yourself to live life once more.

'You want to go to borstal, is that it? You want to be one of the tough kids. You wouldn't stand a second in a place like that. We didn't raise you to see you get sent away to prison. Imagine the shame.'

'You're such a wee snitch running to the teacher to tell tales like that.'

'Why are you so fuckin' shit at everything? You're shit at football and climbing trees and fighting. You're a fucking embarrassment. I don't want to be your friend anymore.'

It always ended in failure. You eventually returned to the ferment of your condition: the impossibility of living and the terror of dying.

The winds are still and the night is silent. A listless cloud moves across the moon and obscures the land. Outside is blackness; the darkest night on earth. He feels its discordant echo through his atomising corpse. His core gradually slipping away. How many hours to the dawn now? Will he witness even that?

The heat is abominable; terrible and terminal in the intensity of its ferocity. There is no molecule of air saved from its potent and vengeful wrath. On every surface there is a ring of humid, fetid moisture. A petri dish of disease and decay. Death and life, birth and renewal; incarnations of water and sunlight combined to create new forms. Even in the hot desert sands, flowers can bloom.

You sat already exhausted in a black leather-and-chrome swivel chair you had rescued from a skip. Your studio space had become smaller and grubbier even than Leith. You missed taking a walk in the afternoons and watching the sea, and the occasional trips along the coast to Portobello Beach. Shoreditch was landlocked, there was a long walk to the Thames and an even longer walk to the sea. Everyone was on the up, except for you. They all knew their place, where they were going, how to get there. They had come from all over, all the top schools and universities. Their names, dates and places were all interchangeable. They had fifty or a hundred ideas a minute and all of them were alleged strokes of genius. They were unfeasibly confident and you wondered how they had gained it all. They hadn't shown, they hadn't been discovered, they weren't represented by any gallery; they were all too good for that. They congratulated one another on everything and nothing. You couldn't comprehend what it was that they did, that they produced. They existed in an invisible force of invincibility, too brilliant to be understood by the ancient regime of cultural barometers. They were there to rip everything up, destroy Jerusalem and build a new Sodom and Gomorrah. You can't recall many of their names now, nobody can.

'We must construct our own deities, just as the ancients did,' one proclaimed.

'The old order is dying. We are the new Barbarians. The Young Turks which will burn their corpses,' blasted another.

'God is dead, Marx is dead, Freud is dead, long live the future.' Typical of their empty sentiments.

They all seemed to know one another, to have studied together under the same tutors. They laughed and joked together constantly, quoting names of contemporaries and art world players I had never heard of. Few, if any, had exhibited outside of art school and yet they knew everyone, attended everything. They huddled together in pubs and bars, restaurants and galleries. I never understood where their income came from; most appeared to simply sign on the dole. They said, get on the lists, go everywhere, meet everyone, network, party, drink free booze and eat free food. They were at some millionaire's pad in Holland Park on a Tuesday night and then they went from there to cash their giro at a Post Office in Hoxton on the Wednesday morning. It was the dawning of a new art movement: a new Bohemia.

She remained in the north and you embedded yourself in the south. Your art worlds were separated by distance and cohesion. Hers was calculated methodically and rationally, yours was all anarchy and chaos. You sheltered at first in a squat with five others, in Islington. Six months later it was being renovated to be transformed into luxury apartments. You hadn't even realised that the building was owned by one of your fellow squatter's parents. Ex-hippies and peaceniks who had joined in the march to progress, reinvented themselves as yuppie property developers, evicted their own child. They even shook hands with you at a preview several years later and bought one of your works; a portrait of a homeless man. You told them you had known their son, then a civil servant, but the irony was lost on them.

'I used to squat in one of your buildings with your son, you know,' I tell them admiringly.

'Which one?' they ask, bemused.

'On Holloway Road in Islington.'

'Oh, we sold that years ago. It was a terrific investment, though.'

I witnessed that face for a long time afterwards. I can vaguely picture it still. In London, in France, in America; all over the world, I never forgot you. Those were lean, dark years, when everything was in flux and nothing was certain. The dynamics of the artistic and cultural landscape and the vicissitudes of the marketplace kept everything in a near-constant state of calamity. People were getting rich, but not me. I felt as though I was becoming increasingly destitute. The cost of everything in London was in permanent continuum skywards; a gilded paradise for those tuned in and connected to the capitalist airwaves; as for the rest of us, it was the law of diminishing returns.

We walked along the beach hand in hand, in the evening, when it was cooler. We observed each other's feet splashing through the crystal-clear ripples of the western Mediterranean. My feet older and hairier than those of the child paddling in the cold, fresh mountain waters, perched upon the stones in the long, twisting glen. Boiled eggs, tomatoes, cheese rolls, packets of crisps, Coca-Cola. A family picnic on the grass in my homeland, bathed in the warm June sunshine. Back at home, in the evening, we had strawberries and ice cream. My father and mother seemed relaxed for once and my brother had temporarily forgotten how much he detested me. Whereas we drank sangria and ate paella, went back to the hotel complex and fooled around. How different and separate life is. Strung together by glimpses of past worlds forgotten or half-remembered. That wasn't me and you; it was me and her, wasn't it? Yet these things I speak of here shall all come to pass. And when we are dead, how will we know ourselves?

The light beckons briefly then fades again in his tiny, cell-like room. The hot, stagnant air rages on as before. His breath paces towards a lull, when finally it will end altogether. Some grains of sand on the window heave themselves onto the floor in the briefest of breezes. The relief of replenished air does not stretch itself as far as his bed. He groans onwards, towards an inevitable fate.

I survived on the streets, in the greasy spoon cafés, in the grubby, run-down pubs, in the crumbling old cinemas, but London was changing; even then, it was constantly in motion. I took my sketchpad and materials everywhere I went; stalking the capital. From discount shops in Hackney to Mayfair galleries, I crisscrossed the city, north and south, east and west. And I drew it, I drew it all. Seven hundred sketches in four months. I documented the seedy streets around King's Cross and the glamorous pavements of Bond Street. I drew the stars in Leicester Square and the rubberneckers in the crowd. The swaying drunks of Soho and the hard-working hostesses. Shoe-gazers and Essex girls, self-conscious on the dance floor. Barmaids, waiters, market porters, and the city boys smug in their suits and Beamers. Policemen on horseback and angry protestors. Au pairs in the parks and vicious-looking pitbulls. Champagne cocktails and rough-sleepers. Half-empty music venues and Christmas shoppers. Bomb blasts and football hooligans. Nurses, tube drivers, bankers, racists and socialists, the strong and the vulnerable. I drew London.

She didn't call you like you thought she would. She didn't beg you to return as you fantasised in your head. You didn't know how she coped. You didn't find out. Even now, you don't know. She married, had children, owns her own gallery. You excused yourself from caring because she was stronger than you. She didn't need your sympathy. You saved all your pity for yourself. Wept at nights in the dark of the squat. Couldn't admit you were wrong. There was always something crippling you. Did you really think they were all better than you, or did you always know that you were the most important person in the room? Something drove you on. You constantly reinvented your circumstances. You never turned back to see what you had left.

How impossible it is to disentangle it all. There is no truth in anything. What should I have said that should have been any different to anything else? How should I have lived a different life? How should I justify my existence? Would another life have been a better life? My brother fat and bloated, a decaying corpse skimming across the waves. My heart broke for a man who hated me. Would he have felt any different if it had been me? My mother and father both dead. How could I have returned to them and asked more of them than they were ever willing to give? Our small family unit was rotten at the centre. There was never more than the promise of what we had. There was never any more love than was already given. No more hope to spare than was shared among us anyway. I knew it wasn't enough, that they could never be enough. My brother's girlfriend had left him before it happened. He must have felt a terrible loneliness out at sea, in that boat, in a storm. Perhaps he knew he would never return to port again. Swallowing a ton of salty water, no longer breathing, passing out into an eternity of blackness, just carrion for all the little creatures roaming the open waves.

I was placed in a group show and then given my own exhibition due to the critical acclaim my work received. I called the show: *Who'll be my Mirror: London through the Eyes of an Outsider*. It was a portrait of an impenetrable, permanently ambivalent world. I drew all over the gallery walls, image upon image, with a cast of hundreds moving constantly in and out of focus. The capital loved it and they came in their ego-driven hordes. Vainly trying to access themselves and their vapid sense of their own entitlement to posterity. I robbed them of their victory; all they could find was a sense of melancholic defeat. A society that had lost all sense of proportionate response to humanity. A greedy, spiteful, superficial and senseless place, and for all the time that has now passed, a feeling I have for London which has endured. But it did have energy; a youthful, ambitious spirit which pervaded through the metropolis, infecting all life surrounding it. A city which was transformative and enabling and produced a magnetising death-grip on the soul.

The art world thawed, the capital opened up. I was able to write a piece on my experience of London for *The Guardian*. I struggled through a thousand words, wishing with every syllable committed that I was with her still. The art was mine, but the text was hers. People said hello to me who had not previously acknowledged my existence. Others crossed vast rooms to shake my hand. I rented a studio and living space near Spitalfields. I had a new London gallery, an art market Svengali behind me, and lots and lots of posh new friends. I was introduced to pop stars, models, fashion designers, architects, musicians, producers, directors, actors, writers, journalists, academics, television presenters, dealers, collectors, curators, gallerists, the hip, the cool, the highly-strung, the shady, the dodgy, the downright criminal; in other terms, the powerful and elite of British culture.

You sweated through the crushing insecurities, lying in your metal cot in the corner of the room you had portioned off for yourself as living quarters. A small gas burner, a kettle, some mugs, a clothes rail, a leather recliner, a battered red velvet sofa, a small bathroom with an ugly, stained plastic shower curtain. The studio was neatly arranged and devoid of any new work. You drank expensive vodka and gin, bought a case of champagne from a vintners in Knightsbridge. Bought a pair of expensive shoes from Savile Row. Fantasised about sitting on the studio floor with an Armani suit on, bare feet, and a paintbrush in your hand. You didn't know who you were or what you should be. You thought of asking your brother for a job on the fishing trawler. You thought of going back home and living with your parents once more. You wanted to ask her advice on everything. Your mother always promised she could get you a job in the supermarket. You could work your way up, become a manager. You had a university degree. You thought of teaching art in secondary schools or sixth-form colleges. You drank and vomited, partied and hibernated reclusively underneath the duvet. The pain burned on in your body and your soul.

'You, work on the boats? Don't be so fucking ridiculous. You wouldn't last cast-off.'

'What do you want me to tell you? That it was the correct decision. Do you want me to draw you a blueprint for how to live your life? How would I know? You have to choose for yourself.'

'All the jobs have gone, son, you're too late. You should have gotten in sooner.'

'Teaching back here? You? You're kidding, right?'

I would wander for days through the National Gallery, staring at painting after painting. Sitting in front of Salvator Rosa's *Witches at their Incantations*. So horrific, so beguiling; a true masterpiece. Everything I sketched appeared so uninspired in response to this great work. Why create art of less import than that of the past? Why not simply stop?

What was it that I possibly had to say?

An expanse of land with an incalculable number of grains of sand, punctuated by rocks and trees. Followed by more land, and more. More of the same; the same texture, the same colour. North, south, west and east dictated solely by the sun. The soil underfoot; ancient, primal, unchanged for millennia. The desert casts its spell long and far.

You crawled away from the world. In the back corner of an empty and lonely studio. You missed her. You could smell her still. You could see her eyes and her smile. You could hear her laugh and her opinions. You missed her positive connection with the world. You could feel her naked body, warm, in bed with yours. You could feel yourself in her. You could view her tears still, after she had tried to help an old man who had fallen in the street and then called her racist epithets rather than receive her help. And the tears she wept, shortly before you left her, when her mother had told her that she had been diagnosed with breast cancer.

I tried to phone once. She had moved on. Gone through to Glasgow to study for an MA and get involved in setting up a new gallery there. Later, after her peregrinations around the world, she moved back to Edinburgh and opened her own gallery. I loved you then and I love you still.

In an empty, soiled bed, I played around with a craft knife. Scratched its blade along my wrists. I couldn't do it; not then, not ever. I waited miserably for the moment that surely must come. A lifetime spent terrified of the only thing guaranteed to actually happen to any individual.

The world came back into focus, it always does. There are phone calls and knocks on the door. There are bills and rents and miscellaneous monies outstanding. None of us are entitled to wallow for long. The kingmakers must have their cut; if not, they'll find a new court jester. I was on advanced warning to shape up and play the part. Wayward genius is one thing, finances are another.

'Dickheads and tossers,' you screamed at the walls. It was no use, you were in their velvet paw and they could claw you to death at any moment. You learned disdain for the critics and the gilded bourgeoisie, mulling around the galleries, pontificating vociferously, slurping cheap wine and munching down pompous canapés. You learned how to play the game and work the room. You learned how to kiss their arses.

'I read the piece you wrote on Egon Schiele. I thought it was fantastic, very insightful. He was a real hero and inspiration of mine at university. He still is, actually.'

'Great book on Bacon. He is absolutely one of my heroes.'

'I learned everything from Picasso, you know, so I'm really looking forward to your monograph.'

The darkness seeps through the door, a shadow crawling surreptitiously and ominously across the floor. Tugging at the hem of his bed, climbing under the sheet to swaddle him in death. He creakingly pants on, his breath a mere murmur in the dense black heart of the universe.

I arose from my grave, cleared the decks, went back to work. I produced two exhibitions nine months apart from each other. The London show was entitled *The Successful Artist* and the other *All You Need is Love*. The second exhibition was put on in a new contemporary gallery in Birmingham. In the gallery's chill-out room, filled with bean bags and bowls of sweets, I painted the walls a thick, tarry black. An old Beatles single rotated on a record player at varying speeds.

You went to Los Angeles for the first time; a shapeless, shifting city, its hallucinatory freeways snaking through the night. By day, a thick smog covered the flat, grimly twinkling metropolis. From up in the canyons, you could watch the pollution descend and the throbbing heat rise. It was as though hell had finally taken root on earth and was punishing all the denizens of the valley below for their undisclosed sins. You drove along Santa Monica Boulevard in a white limo. It was a trashy, tacky town with not a piece of tinsel, nor an angel, to be found anywhere. But you did discover the Pacific Ocean: cool, blue and shimmering in the most gorgeous halo of sunshine you had ever seen.

A new impresario was taking over, switching funds from the stock market into the art market. New York was already sewn up, but LA was wide open. At least it was back then. He later franchised out all over the globe. I was at the opening some years later, of his North London, minimalist-designed hangar. Christ, what a space. It took me six weeks' constant graft just to fill the walls with drawings in one of the two smaller gallery spaces. He bought everything. They said there was half a billion dollars' worth of art in his Upper East Side penthouse. A stocky man, with thick white hair, constantly trimmed, he wore nothing but black. He was married to the heiress of a nationally operated air-conditioning manufacturer. They said that's where he got his start, with her money. They also said he was gay. If he was, he didn't show it; not openly, anyway. He was a progressively-minded registered Democrat, who helped fill the party's war chest every presidential election. He threw fundraisers for candidates. He was also a fully pledged philanthropist. He had a daughter he loved, trapped in a wheelchair, and a son that he loathed; a drunken, drug-addled playboy fornicator. A man who frittered his time away on yachts in the Aegean with supermodels and other over-pampered wasters like himself. I met the son twice and liked him immediately. The daughter would take over the dynasty and indulge her sibling as her mother was wont to do. The daughter was the true power and brains in the family. She was the one all the artists cultivated. Her tastes were definitive and final. You were either in or you were out. I was always in. She seemed to like me. I never quite took to her, though. I thought she had too much clout in the marketplace and too much say in the art world in general. Her politics may have been pinko, but her will was a rod of iron: cold, hard and unbending. Many an artist starved because of her.

'I'm going to make sure you're solidly blue chip, that all our artists are. My mission in life is to bring the people art; great art.' She sits in a wheelchair, her legs paralysed. She is indomitable.

The ocean and the sky had a profound effect on me. I should never have left them. I froze in the gaze of their beauty and luminance. I could have existed within them. Let myself simply be. I needed nothing else. The warm, tender hand of the universe on my face. The sand underneath me, blessing my body. Nature would provide for everything. Is this what the pioneers felt as they travelled as far west as they could come? The sea, the blue, the sky, the mountains, the green, the sun, the canyons, the yellow, the beaches, the orange, the cliffs, the coast: God's great and bountiful earth beneath their feet. Why did I ever return to the world? I should have disappeared into that golden sunlight as it set down over the endless expanse of the Pacific ocean.

The LA show was simply an introduction to some rehashed ideas. I would always reimagine previous work for Los Angeles exhibitions. I already had a foot in the door and didn't need to convince anyone. Angelenos were delighted to have recycled art presented to them. It's what they existed with all the time in the entertainment industry. Which is where most of the city's inhabitants that I met worked. They wanted art for the walls of their gloomy Spanish-style villas. Many of them appeared to hate the light and lived in houses which were dark and filled with cold air fed from air-conditioning units. They didn't seem very keen on the heat, either. Especially those who had vacated there from the East Coast and bitched permanently about the unchanging seasons. I liked LA for all of the reasons they seemed to hate it and disliked it for all of the reasons that they seemed to love it.

Still, I found London a dispiriting and depressing city to return to. The heavy walls of the studio were cold and damp and the denizens of the capital all appeared lobotomised, on an endless treadmill of wealth creation. I drank myself into a stupor for two days, which, mixed in with the jetlag, meant I stayed in bed for a week.

You never liked London. You appreciated everything it had to offer over everywhere else, but you never ever settled there. You always blamed it for the end of your relationship with her. You thought you should have stayed in Edinburgh and lived a smaller life: working, exhibiting, living. You could have been closer to your parents, attended their funerals. You could have become a national cause for celebration in the art world. Instead, you became estranged from your own country and were never a full player in its cultural dialogue with itself. You were always referred to as a British artist, or Scottish-born artist, never a Scottish artist. You never did exhibit there again.

I can't feel the cold of my country anymore. My home town, like some small model trapped inside a little globe, snow falling upon snow, at the end of the universe. I can hardly remember any of it now. A sense of place lost forever; in fact, lost a long time ago.

The heat and the dust lay still on the desert floor. The herdsmen and their cattle sleep on, oblivious to this stranger's impending death. Perhaps they dream of their homes; of their families; of their children; of their wives. Out here under the stars, the nocturne breathes on and the earth keeps spinning.

A collector lent you an apartment in Rome, off the Via Veneto, just round the corner from the Excelsior Hotel. There was a central drawing room, its walls newly white-washed and bare. You stayed for a whole summer. It was the last independent commission you undertook. In the bedroom there was a mattress. It's all you required. You drank cappuccino for breakfast, ate street food for lunch: pizza and calzone. For dinner you ate pasta at cheap trattorias: *penne all'arrabiata, spaghetti pomodoro, spaghetti alle vongole, spaghetti aglio, olio, e pepperoncino, spaghetti carbonara.* You listened endlessly to Frank Sinatra, Dean Martin, Tony Bennett, and lots of opera records, which you never could stand. In the humid evening air you went for a *passeggiata* and ambled down to your favourite *gelateria*, for pistachio and *stracciatella*. The heat drove you crazy and you often worked naked, taking short breaks to drink espressos from a stove-top pot. Bottles and bottles of San Pellegrino were your constant companion. You drank wine on Saturday nights and masturbated on Sundays.

He was a businessman, who owned a few electronics companies, two racehorses, and was alleged to be the biggest producer of pornography in Italy. I called the piece: *Intimations*. I covered his walls in Italian Cinema: Fellini, Pasolini, Rosselini, Visconti, Antonioni, De Sica; stars, scenes, audiences, humour, laughter, pain, suffering, pathos, redemption, death and salvation. I used inks and paints to make it permanent. I don't know what he did with it, I never saw it again after I had finished. He had viewed some initial sketches I had worked up beforehand and had approved them. He paid my commission to the gallery, after a few months of wrangling, by which time I was back in London and didn't give a fuck any more, about him or the work. It was some derivative drivel I had knocked together. The whole thing was simply an opportunity to gather myself together and regroup. He passed himself off as an *haute bourgeoisie* intellectual but in reality he was smuggling girls into Europe and virtually enslaving them in the sex industry. I heard rumours about his nefarious activities at the time, found out for certain later, when his body was discovered in the boot of a car, in a back street in Milan. He had been shot twice in the head. Nobody seemed surprised, least of all my gallery.

Was it at a party or a club where I first met you? I had seen you before in someone's performance piece. Your beautiful face and contorted body were all I had to stop myself from drifting off into a coma. Still, I can't see the place now where we met, or what we first said. We must have been introduced, I wouldn't have spoken to you otherwise. I took you for a model; you were an actress. You were always an actress, right to the very last. We met for a drink in a bar in Soho, then caught a cab to a restaurant in Mayfair; popular at the time with celebrities, though I don't recall seeing any. You walked and talked like a star most of the time anyway, at least in public.

'I hate these dreary streets around here, all old money replaced by *nouveau riche*. What's the difference, I ask you? They're much of the same ilk, their tired tropes, listless parties and pointless orgies. Wasteful degenerates any decent revolutionary party would execute in a second. Quite right too, don't you think?' She embarks on the topic exquisitely.

'Sure, I'm all for murdering the police and burning the rich.' I shrug.

She stands still, shocked, and stares at me.

'Now you're not one of these little coffee shop communists are you? Some dirty, Stalinist apologist pamphleteer?' she inquires haughtily.

'Who, me? Not at all. I am but a humble nihilist,' I soothe.

'Good god, they're the worst. To not believe in anything at all.' She squeals to the rooftops.

'Well I do believe in something.'

'Just what, exactly?'

'Nihilism,' I state resoundingly.

You wore a necklace which you claimed was made of real diamonds, that a dead, aristocratic great aunt had left you in her will, due to her appreciation and delight at your ballet skills as a child. She had dreamed of the ballet for herself, but had been forced to marry some dull little smallholder in South Wales. You later admitted that the diamonds were in fact fake, but never spoke of the great aunt. We ate and we drank, we caught a cab to your shared flat in Paddington, and I spent the night with you. You cared little for the same social graces as others. I paid for the meal and you extravagantly tipped the taxi driver twenty pounds. The flat was a jumble of unhanged pictures, books, records, plays, scripts, dirty pans, an old, stolen, black-and-white television, and a 1920s gramophone. There was what appeared to be a genuine fox-fur stole hanging up in the hallway. We went to your bedroom, stumbled around a little drunkenly, before you sat on the bed and called me to you. We kissed passionately for a moment, before you unzipped me and began sucking my cock; then you pushed a finger up my arse and I came immediately. When my rational senses returned, I was in shock. You had vacated the bedroom for the bathroom, so I quickly and silently pulled my shorts and trousers back up, then sat down on a worn wicker chair. When you returned to the room you were smiling coyly. You never said anything at first and neither did I. Then you enquired as to what we should do next. We retired to bed for the night and fucked twice, then once more in the morning for good measure. Why, with you, did we always make love but with her we always fucked? Where was the emotional connection? I never wanted it again really. Not after witnessing a corpse. I can smell her still, that earthy smell of her sex, the exquisite perfumes she always wore: the silk, satin, lace, leather, rubber, PVC, fur; the shampoo that smelt of bubble gum, the bath salts which smelled of pink grapefruit, tangerines and lavender; the bourbon and Bordeaux; the chilli, lemon and garlic chicken she would make. We never just had sex, we always rutted like wild animals.

You could have it then, a girl like her. Success had changed you, as it changes everyone. You were a star and she wasn't, but she was the one that acted like she was. You played her strange games. You played them all. You amused others, later, regaling them with some of her exploits, but not all of them. Many you kept for yourself. Late night assignations that seemed to have happened to someone else and so they were no longer your stories to tell. Others you fantasised about right up to the end. In the darkness, the loneliness, the despair, at coming down, drying out, sobering up. You played them again for comfort and for sexual satisfaction. Did you dream her? Imagine her? She ended up for a time on an American daytime soap, then disappeared forever into the vastness of the hinterland of the Wild West frontier. You heard she was a high-class hooker in Phoenix, Arizona; a transgender, burlesque dancer in Las Vegas; an English professor in Ithaca, New York; or else she was a film producer in Canada. The most probable sighting was as a bar manager in San Francisco. You looked in once, when you were in that city, but they had never heard of her.

The sound of a wild animal penetrates the walls of his room. He cannot place the position of the noise nor its circumstances for being. Is it a creature of the night who has killed, or is being killed? He grips the beaten mattress and weeps for his physical state of utter decline. He will join the animal quarry in that vast, sand wilderness soon enough.

In your periodic fast and abstinences you went to a local gym in the early morning, with the hardcore athletic types getting their power-run in before a day of drudgery at the office. You ran with a flaccid, carefree stride; the same one you had always used, even as a child. Most of the others could run faster in the races. There was one other child who had a partial disability, or was partly crippled, as they said back then. You felt a heel beating him all the time and so you let him win once. He milked it for all it was worth, putting you down at every turn, laughing with the same classmates that called him spaz behind his back and sometimes to his face. You hated him for it, you hated yourself for it, and you hated the world for it.

'He can't even outrun a spastic like me,' he tormented you gleefully, hamming it up for the enveloping crowd.

There was a point in the day, or else the week, when I bested them all. When the art materials came out. I was more creative than all of them put together and they knew it. Some showed appreciation, some asked for tuition, many remained silent. The occasional boy pontificated on the appreciation of physical feats of strength and endurance and the derision of artistic acumen. Though never the toughest boys, nor the best athletes. Neither had to prove themselves to anybody, they already existed in an external state of fêted exuberance and fearful loathing.

'That's really good, I wish I could draw like that.'

'Will you show me how to do that?'

'What can you do with drawing? You're better being a footballer, or a boxer, they get loads of money and tons of birds.'

It was all so exhausting in the end. A lifetime of proving yourself. Wanting that acclaim, achieving those rewards; and for who, and for what? In that moment, at my own insistence, I recognised it was all so terribly disappointing. I finally accepted that state of melancholy; the purest sense of being. When the world offers itself up to us as though for the first time and in that same instant we recognise our own mortality. The door opens and closes with the very same movement.

She broke up the monotony of the day in the studio. The tawdry, sleazy nights rampaging through the city. She offered sensual longing and sexual pleasures beyond anything I had ever experienced. They said she had once been a courtesan for rich Arab millionaires. They said she had been raised in a circus in Hungary. That her mother had been the lover of European royalty, both male and female. That her father had been the head torturer for Franco. They were, of course, all lies. Though what the exact truth is, I couldn't claim to know. She was young, she was beautiful, and she was sexually omnivorous, ravenous and rapacious. She lived her life with a bohemian abandon and intensity. I delighted in every moment spent with her, but wished to spend no more time with her than was prudent. After our sessions together I always crawled back home ravaged and empty: a sexual haemophiliac. It was all so unreal, as though a page torn from an adult fairy tale. I had no notion of anything other than work and our time together; the real world existed outside of that. She was my Baudelairean Vampiress and I willingly gave myself to her, body, but not soul.

'She works for the Russians, you know,' a part-time art dealer once declared of her.

'Her ex-boyfriend and she were involved in some business

selling small arms to the Saudis. Apparently they made a real killing on one trade, a deal that was only too good to be true, because he ended up dead in mysterious circumstances,' yet another claimed with regard to her burgeoning biography.

'She plays the tables at a Mayfair casino like a Stradivarius.' One of the more banal pieces of conjecture surrounding her.

The market never stands still, it never procrastinates, and it never sentimentalises anything. It is a monster which feeds on the young, the strong, the talented and the saleable with equal voracity. It employs all measures at its means to connive, coerce and capitalise on every nuance of every niche in a never-ending zeitgeist. It needs souls, lots of them, and its satanically-tended scythe harvests them endlessly. There is no escape, there are no reprieves, the market retains constant indomitability. Art is a commodity like all others and artists are mere slaves to the process. As one exits the meat grinder, entirely eviscerated, another enters it.

Your loathing grew exponentially with each exhibition, meeting, interview, preview, dinner party. You began to detest them all. You especially began to detest yourself. The constant capitulation to their tastes, their needs, their requirements, was murdering your own innate sense of your artistic worth and value and that of you as a unique human being. You drifted away from the quotidian, searching for other life. You found it, in an unlikely guise, on the streets.

How did I get here? To this place where I am to die. Over seas and mountains, rivers and lakes, borders and countries, valleys, plains and deserts. I do not know its name, nor what the people call themselves.

The cattle startle and the herdsmen jump awake; alert, staffs at the ready, to defend themselves and their precious livestock. An unidentified animal moves in the distance, out of sight from their prowling eyes. They watch, listen, smell the air, with its humming heat, bearing down all around. The danger passes, the cattle settle, the herdsmen bed down once more, sleeping with one eye open.

He cannot move, breathe evenly, nor feel the space surrounding him. His lungs have contracted; his heart has reduced its function of pushing blood around his hollow veins. The room is bathed in a darkness blacker than he has ever known. Everywhere, there is the silence of a life extinguishing out into the boundlessness of an infinite nothing. Life: an interlude between void and void. Stagnantly weary, he mimics weeping for an existence now passing. For the moments that have passed, the moments that should have been, and the moments that will never come. The horror of being has relentlessly taken root in his fading consciousness. He feels the end within him, its inevitability and its impossibility.

Did I ever feel a heat so intense and a cold so chilling to the bones? I will never visit my country again. My ancestors remain buried among the mountains and lochs, the rivers and glens, in a cold and damp land. I will join them soon enough, in a blanket of emptiness that sings out across all time and all epochs.

We were fighting for our future freedoms; that's what I was advised, anyway. Friends persuaded me out of my political apathy and slumber to join forces with them on a series of demonstrations and happenings. I made some art for the collective endeavour, *gratis*. My gallery was sceptical and apprehensive; the resulting infamy could go one of two ways. I argued my case and played both sides. I had little interest in either and feigned my commitment to both.

She couldn't have been more than twenty, or twenty-one. An anarchist grouping were getting increasingly agitated over police intrusion into what was a peaceful and fun demonstration. The police snapped, some young and inexperienced officers too pumped-up on adrenaline, aggression and an overriding sense of pure moral authority, broke ranks and began attacking the demonstrators. The revellers fought back and a melee ensued. Some young woman, unknown to me, pushed an officer away from an injured comrade; the officer then let full rein with his baton, hitting her repeatedly on the body and then twice in the head. She spent six weeks in a coma before dying, and I witnessed it all.

You didn't do anything. You froze, blinded by the sudden violence, by the sudden engagement with a passive situation. You were bored, thinking of scurrying away, drifting off to the pub. It was so strange and unreal, more so when you kept playing it back in your mind for days afterwards. When you were later called to the enquiry your recollection differed from all of the others, as they indeed did from each in their own turn.

Her body lay there like a ragdoll; lifeless, impassive. The officer disappeared into the throngs of the blue line, I never recognised him. The Met were allegedly filming, but missed that incident; both sides did. There was a demonstration against police brutality after her funeral had taken place. The atmosphere was tense, violent, filled with hate. I was there. I've never forgiven him for what he did; not only to her, but to me. He changed me forever, for better and for worse, and in ways I didn't comprehend then. When I returned fully to that moment, that incident, for the first time in my life I felt truly sad. It shook the foundations of every truth I accepted as granted in life. It was an absolute refusal of freedom, by the state, by the powerful, to the weak. I realised what they could take away from me: everything. That they could do it to me and that they could do it to everyone else. That they needed no permission. The enquiry acquitted the officer in question and that was the end of the matter.

I wondered what went on in her mind as she lay on a hospital bed, paralysed and unconscious. Did her subconscious continue? Did it replay moments from the history of her young life? Did it resurrect joys and triumphs, defeats and disappointments? Did it contain nightmares of another world created in the ether of her fragmented mental capacities? Did she see monsters and devils, a kaleidoscope of insanity, of which there was no escape but for death? I created my next exhibition from these factors: *Mysteries of a Life Past*. It wasn't a political work but a strange, hypnotic and hallucinatory journey into an unravelling mind.

Members of the dead girl's family attended the show. They left deflated and unimpressed, wondering what such abstract notions conveyed about who she really was and the issues which she was committed to and ultimately died for. They asked you, through the surrogate medium of the press, what you knew of causes and the reasons people fought for them. They accused you of simply piggybacking on a sensational news story to further your own artistic career.

'What has the narcissism of this young man's art got to do with our daughter's death, or even, for that matter, with her life?' the family were quoted as saying.

'It wasn't supposed to be a realist vision of what happened. I wasn't looking to represent the verisimilitude version of physical events. But an abstracted and deconstructed psychological dementia obtained through these events,' I stated in response.

You justified yourself lamely and your gallery had to step in to contain the fallout and in the process secure you more publicity for the exhibition.

She worked on and off as an actress; small parts in television, a couple of unmemorable film roles in low budget, East End, gangster-geezer fair. Her great love was the theatre. I was reliably informed that she was good, but always by men who seemed to covet her. She was always very selective in her romances but as far as I could tell she was highly competent at her craft. She had performed in some Shakespeare, Chekhov and Ibsen. Her other credits included *Juno and the Paycock*, *No Exit*, *Look Back in Anger*, and an improvisational student production of *Marat/Sade* using only three actors. At the time of our meeting she was up for a part in a revival of Jean Genet's *The Maids*, which she didn't get. I never saw or heard from her for a week after that. She played in her own performance of the dying swan in bed for several days after the rejection. She never appeared to do anything other than act to earn money. I never witnessed any truth in the many rumours surrounding her. I once asked her what she saw in me. She answered that I was cute, in a guy kind of way, talented, and, she believed, deeply authentic. Perhaps she just saw something in me, a willingness to be led down the rabbit hole by her. She was nothing if not dramatic.

The first of your games with her was strange, intense, exhilarating and confusing. She asked you to undress outside her room and when she called out to say she was ready, for you to knock on the door. You did so and she sternly replied to enter. She sat on the bed dressed as a Victorian governess; a white, high-collared shirt, a long black skirt with black leather lace-up boots poking out from underneath. She wore black silk gloves and her long red hair up in a bun. In her right hand she gripped a cane. She called you to her and you went tentatively. Those few steps impenetrable, until you reached her. She placed your naked body over her knees, then whispered in your ear that the safe word was 'marzipan'. She asked you to repeat it, but your mouth was dry and your throat hoarse. She asked you again and you spoke that odd and pointless word. You didn't remember ever having been beaten before. It was so archaic, awkward and laughable, then she struck you. You let out a formless word: a flinching of pain. Further strokes arrived and your buttocks became inflamed. You asked her to stop and she merely thwacked you again. Then it dawned on you that marzipan was real, it was a proper word, with genuine effects. You spat the word out hastily before she could strike you again. Instead, she stroked your face and told you that you had been a good boy. That you would get your reward. She lay back and placed your head up her skirt. She was wearing stockings and nothing else. You knew what she wanted, but she commanded you anyway. After a few moments she placed you on your back, raised her skirt and clamped your arms in between her legs and made you perform until she had her orgasm. She stayed in position, putting her hand back and making you hard. She then shifted herself down and slowly, teasingly, sat on you and fucked you ravenously.

'Marzipan, marzipan, marzipan, marzipan.' What a strange and delightful word.

The pleasure of climax was extraordinary; she was beautiful, desirable, dominant. I wanted nothing else in the world but to be there with her forever. This strange apparition of an anachronistic caricature, a stock character in her formidable repertoire. I could view her on top of me, cold and aloof, and I could smell her, all over my mouth and chin, earthy and feminine. She broke into a smile, bent over, and kissed me tenderly. She was the most free person I ever met.

I stayed the night then drifted out into the foggy dawn of the city before she had awoken. It was a shocked landscape, the beginnings of a new day, everything calm and ordered and serene. A minimal version of the beating, chaotic metropolis. It was a slightly surreal sight, the streets appeared drunken and out of focus. There was a hush of noise as though I was still lying asleep in her bed. It was a Sunday morning and I caught a tube homewards to the studio. The station and carriage were quiet, placated perhaps by the *sturm und drang* of the night before.

I arrived at the studio that morning desolate and debauched. I didn't go to bed, instead I put a pot of coffee on the stove top and began to work. I set to the task of individual works collectively titled: *Secrets*. I drew a dead, naked man being spanked over the knee of a live, naked woman in a funeral parlour. I drew a young, bourgeois pair chatting amiably in a high-tech kitchen, glasses of champagne in their hands, while through the wall their spouses were having sexual relations; she on her knees performing fellatio while pushing a large dildo up his anus: his face contorted with agony and ecstasy.

A giant octopus slithers along the walls and the ceiling of the bedroom. It detaches its suckers from the plaster and falls onto you. At its core is an enormous vagina which contracts and expands at will. It clamps itself onto your face and smothers you. The tentacles wrap themselves around your body. The vagina forms itself deeper and heavier around your entire head. You cannot breathe. You gasp for air. You slowly begin to asphyxiate. Your penis hardens and becomes monstrously tumescent. It explodes suddenly and sperm covers the walls, dripping down like gloopy stalactites onto the now detached and flaccid octopus corpse.

You drew to escape the pain. That's why you kept seeing her. To live in a separate world away from the corruption and injustice. To avoid the social and political chaos at the beating heart of the planet; a stain which soils all. You drew for shock value, to *épater la bourgeoisie*, for money, for notoriety, for fame, for anything other than the truth. You drew to escape your growing sense of obligation towards your fellow human beings. The series got you noted. It got you commissions. It changed the direction your art would take.

That emptiness began to seep in even then; a kind of despair at the world. A recognition that my place would always be on a temporal fringe. A solitary man interacting with the various stratums of society, but never belonging to any one community. Useful only in the purposefulness for which I could negotiate, the vested interest in me and my talents, by whomsoever required them. Beyond the physical, it's what I discovered in her; the ability to live her life as she saw fit, without intervention by others. Her dramas and crises she invented for herself, for her own amusement. She was not without sympathy, empathy or humanity. She was tolerant to an absolute fault, and a more deeply sensitive person than I ever was. I couldn't love her, no matter how much I tried - she was simply an obsession; unique, intense, fleeting.

The air is saturated with a floating veil of mist, all sweat and moisture, stolen from his stagnant body and the damp walls of his abandoned room. The corporeal self has capitulated to time and biology, it no longer functions as a unifying entity for the intrinsic sense of a physical being. It is unbounded, detached, making its resting space as the terroir for the soul.

The red ripples in the sunset sands appear black now under the moon. It lays the desert landscape into a carapace of texture, tone, light and shadow. A darkness burning on through the night until the golden light of dawn seeps across the gently illuminating dunes.

How different it was from those glazed-over eyes. A voluptuous yet empty existence, devoid of romance, with only fleeting moments of tenderness. Was that how she wanted it? I never asked her, nor offered anything different. Perhaps they were all the same for her. We drank at that deep, fervent well, then left sated: discourteous thieves disappearing into the night.

My gallery admonished me for being too prolific, they posited that it undervalued, or devalued, my work; or something along those lines. I used the downtime to move studio and abode to south of the river. I washed up in Southwark and I managed to locate a studio space in an old abandoned industrial building, once used for plastic moulding, then derelict, but swiftly gentrified for creative types like myself. I also got a mortgage for a flat nearby. I tried to distance myself from you, from the memory of you. The knowledge you were only a train journey away, up north in Scotland. The realisation even then that my life could have turned out to be so much different than it was, but then I was always me; that never changed.

I sat at the bar in a Park Lane hotel, a glass of Rioja in my hand. You walked in and sat at a table. You wore a long brown fur coat, which you later claimed to be real, but I couldn't tell. Your hair was unfurled and your lips were the reddest I had ever witnessed. Your heels were flashy and there was a diamond anklet around your right ankle. The waiter brought you a cocktail which you drank slowly. You came to the bar and whispered the number of the room in my ear. I wandered nervously along the corridor to the door. When you opened it wide and stood pruriently within its frame I realised for the first time that you were naked underneath the coat. I paid you two hundred pounds for a night of passion like no other I had ever experienced. In the morning we went separate ways in our respective taxis, you to Paddington and me to Southwark. You never kept the payment entirely for yourself. A week later you treated me to a show-stopping meal in a Michelin-starred restaurant. You left a hefty tip and even spared some change for a homeless man outside. For you, the real payment was the thrill. As for me, I would have paid you two thousand pounds for that night.

How empty I've often felt. Disenfranchised from my own existence. Separate from all others. Unable to meet that chasm even through art: that which I placed all my faith in. How solitary she made me feel.

Smoking joint after joint in the studio, with Pink Floyd's *The Wall* constantly on repeat, you were aware of how little you had travelled from Leith. You could wander down to the river and view the city of London in all its vainglorious splendour. Your passport was now well-thumbed, but it felt as though nothing had passed. Your new studio walls were bare. There was money in the bank and resentment in your heart.

I am forever here; into eternity we roam, an endless speck of cosmic debris. I will remain one with the universe: thirteen billion years of infinity.

The dark of the night rages onwards, its silence cleansing all. The heat which encloses all depresses the nocturnal spirits. A new day will dawn and the new sun will burn all in its wake. Its rays seeking out every crevice of shadow, to obliterate all relief from its indomitable power.

There was always a sense in your heart that the abyss was chasing after you. You were always on the cusp of capitulation with it. That baroque bohemian experience, that you were never a natural at. Was it solipsistic posturing? Was it simply loneliness? You crawled towards it in evident horror. Drinking champagne for breakfast in the studio on a dank winter's day. Wasn't that London? Wasn't that the great artist in the immense metropolis where all lifestyles were acceptable? The *avant-gardiste*, the experimentalist, the rebel, the non-conformist. Wasn't that what art and the big city was all about? Isn't that the attitude that everyone aspired to?

She took me to an outré new fetish club over in Vauxhall. She dressed provocatively in a tight black rubber dress and PVC high-heeled shoes. I went as myself, but as a concession put on a red leather collar she had surreptitiously brought along for me in her handbag. She waltzed me through the club holding her right index finger through a silver D ring on the collar. We drank, we danced, we laughed, we took poppers and a little cocaine, chatted to some cool, fun people and a few exotic cats, who seemed very committed to the lifestyle. We caught a taxi home to her place at five in the morning, fucked ferociously, and then slept for eighteen hours solid. When we finally hit daylight on Monday lunchtime we had a sweet, innocent lunch date at a pizzeria in Notting Hill before she demurely pecked me on the cheek and dashed off into the ether for an audition for some part in a TV drama; a part which she got. I didn't see her for another six weeks.

I had few ideas and no focus, but the dead activist still haunted me. My worst nightmare was to become some social-realist, girl-meets-tractor bore. More a political polemicist than an artist. Dogmatically peddling some right-on rhetoric about the New Left and the possibilities of world revolution in a rapidly digitising world. I simply wanted to get pissed. I told myself tall tales of genius in my more euphoric moments and self-lacerated in my darkest doubts about myself, and humanity as a whole. My studio remained a minimalist paradise, with three sets of neatly stocked architect drawers, filled with various types and gauges of paper. I had two large desks opposite each other in the centre of the room, three swivel chairs, two drawing boards, cupboards filled with art materials: inks, paints, charcoals, graphite, and a large bookshelf half-filled with a burgeoning array of art books. I bought three new titles a week. There was a large, red, comfortable sofa in the corner for napping. I spent my days getting stoned in the studio and nights getting drunk in the pub. I ate endless takeaways: burgers and fries, kebabs, Chinese, Indian, Thai, sushi, pizza, and a great baked lasagne from a little local Italian around the corner. I watched the sky rise and fall: grey, puce, black, purple, lemon and orange. Rain pounded a skylight, creating a soundscape both enchantingly melancholic and infuriatingly rhythmic. I floated delirious through the city; from exhibition openings to previews, I insisted on viewing them all, constantly on guard against any interlopers to my kingdom: many and frequent. People asked me what I was working on and I learned to lie like a true professional.

'What is it you're up to at the moment? You've moved studio, haven't you? South of the river, I heard.' A fellow artist. The question weighted with the sly subterfuge of the usurper.

'It's been a nightmare, arranging everything. The studio's four times bigger than the last one. It's a far bigger canvas to take on ever greater commissions and *grands projets*.' I fluff my feathers and sharpen my CV in response.

You could assert all the claims you wished. They would never view the work and never care. I feigned bravado, despondency, anguish, circumspection, stoicism and eccentricity. The public simply wanted drama: shock and depravity. They required everything of their artists by proxy.

When I next met her it was in a fashionable new bar over my side of the river. Her hair was now platinum-blonde, which she said was required for a future part in a film, playing a femme fatale. A role, I suspect, she thought she was born for. She looked stunning and remarkably unattainable in deep red lipstick, a figure-hugging long red dress with black faux fur collar and cuffs, a long black leather coat, and, as I discovered later, a pair of high-heeled, black leather over-the-knee boots and no knickers. She caught all the boys' eyes and a few of women's too, but she was loyal and attentive to me. When we left she asked to view my studio. I gave her a guided tour in less than ten minutes, then we opened a bottle of Pol Roger. She flirted and teased even more than usual, before we christened the red sofa. I can still smell the pure animal sex of her. More female than anyone else I ever met. She screwed with every ounce of her body, impetuous, unbounded and uninhibited.

You accepted her, but you never reasoned out why. What was it you had that she desired? Even your career was going stale. You could never have allowed yourself to love such a woman. She would always hold the balance of power, even though she was not controlling in any way. She left you alone to simply be. You demanded nothing of each other and in your own ways remained very private together.

'I like to fuck you.' She speaks hushed and seductively. 'I like your masculinity and your vulnerability. It makes me feel desirable and powerful. I like to be in control. I love to dominate, but not always.'

'It's okay with me,' you stutter out in awed excitement.

She disappeared off into the night, before the dawn broke: a modern-day Cinderella. In the emerging light of the new day a half-empty bottle and two wine glasses sat on top of one of the drawing tables. There were some recently-made stains on the sofa. I smelt their animal scent, both mine and hers. I could still smell her perfume, she always wore such gorgeous perfumes, and her leather coat, and I could still taste the lipstick stain she left on my lips and the blood from when she bit them.

I began a new series of drawings, which eventually became prints for a limited edition book, which my gallery produced, titled: *Her*. It was only a small run of one hundred copies, but it was a premier quality edition, it was expensive, and sold out quickly. Then the gallery, elated at the success of the book, exhibited the original drawings in a show titled: *She*. All the works in the exhibition sold straight off the shelf. She never came to see the show, we were no longer together by then, nor even by the time I had finished the book. She was gone out of my life forever and I out of hers. I don't know what she would have thought of it. We never discussed art much. I sketched her from memory: beautiful, radiant, tender, vulnerable. In many ways how I still view her now, in contradiction to who she was, or who she presented herself to be.

He has limited movement, atrophy has finally set in. He is overwhelmed by a sense of all-pervading darkness, from both within and outside of the self. The mind flickering onwards, images streamed through a dying subconscious.

The crumbling walls creak and crackle in the baking heat of his sealed-in tomb. In the stifling air outside, the night crawls on, the nocturnal grumblings grinding out their final efforts. The desert still and motionless but for the migrations of small grains of sand. Its residents hidden from view. The herdsmen sleep on, the cattle sleep on, the villagers sleep on. A continuation of life everlasting.

You walked through the world, unheralded, triumphant, a passive being thrown open to the vicissitudes of life. You allowed yourself to be swept along in your advancements, with neither fortune nor favour abated. You cursed, harangued, berated yourself and others all through the journey. Your instants of cowardice were staggering, your unflinching willingness to confront truth transcendent. For you, drawing was existing: an excavation of the soul. The rest were moments, relations, rendezvous between separate beings clawing to be united, distressed by their failures to connect sufficiently. We are alone in the self, the first-ever true realisation you encountered in the universe.

An old friend washed up from university days, scrounging after an investment in his nascent, start-up internet venture, selling art. He had disavowed painting in the interests of bringing culture to the masses and making a profit for himself. He needed financial partners and I seemed to have sufficient kudos for him to target me. I invested a small but significant amount and became a shareholder, or stockholder, or something of that nature. The yield would give me a net gain of X percent. My accountant thought it a prudent enough punt and so I lent my old comrade some cash.

'It's a win-win deal. The world is changing irrevocably. The market is wide fucking open, pal. The digitisation and globalisation of business is upon us. Somebody's going to get in there first and make a killing and so it may as well be us. What do you say, are you in or out? I need an answer quick to expedite this situation. We're going to be fucking rich, man,' he states enthusiastically, slapping my arm, all comradely.

'I thought I already was,' I answer facetiously.

In celebration, he invited me along to a party held by some minor rock star who he was also tapping for an investment and an endorsement in his digital enterprise. It was the usual lame affair, attended by a cavalcade of B-listers, hangers-on, and wannabes. There was one welcome and unusual addition.

It seems the rock star and I had two people in common; my old college pal and my drug dealer. We never alluded as to how we really knew each other. He vaguely mentioned writing a few articles on me for a niche magazine. It was actually the truth. My friend was entirely immune as to the provenance of anyone's income, he was only interested in the issue of whether they could invest some of it in his burgeoning company. I left them to discuss market forces, profits and losses, long-term gains and the like, and ran straight into her. She was with a friend, a female friend, that she appeared to be intimate with. She introduced me, we chatted, I sensed my awkward presence. We never established we were lovers in her company, nor that they were in mine. Though that's what I believed them to have been. I made a dignified retreat and allowed them their privacy. They left the party soon after; as did I, alone.

You were disconsolate. You argued with yourself, wrestled with your natural instincts. You were drunk almost continuously for three days. You envisioned them together, they repulsed you, they attracted you. The fantasy wouldn't rescind. She was teasing and tormenting you. Did she do it deliberately, or was it serendipity? You wanted to know. Was this her absent housemate? Were they lovers? Did she fuck her like she fucked you? The presence of your old friend erupted memories of her and your heart ached all over again. Was she the riposte to that, all lust and no love?

She is swathed in a long red leather trench coat which flaps open behind her to reveal her brown and naked body. She totters across the paint-spattered wood flooring in red high heels. She is you, but you are not meant to be her. You bite and nip your teeth into my body. I smell your perfume. You say it's not yours but hers. You slap me hard across my thigh and point across the room. I walk to the sink unit and open the cupboard door underneath. She is there, cramped inside, making love with another woman. I stare at myself and see foam gargling around my lips as the vomit gags up in my mouth.

I didn't ask after you. I never asked him anything about you. He ventured nothing, perhaps so embroiled in his financial ramblings. I did it for you, invested in him. You had always found him amusing and not such a bad painter, either. He had reached the limits of his talent and peaked early. He had stated as such, in a rare moment of gravity for him. He knew his ascent as an artist would never rise above a certain gradient, so he decided to invest in other artists for a profit and a place in the sunshine. I admired him for his lucidity and grew to respect him for his honesty. My gallery wouldn't allow me to sell work through his website, but that didn't seem to cause any acrimony between us. He paid back the dividends and more. Became a multi-millionaire and made others, such as me, a tidy pile of cash on the way. Of course, he lost it all later, when the company crashed and burned. He was declared bankrupt but somehow washed up in Asia, speculating on the markets there and ending up with a second fortune, even greater than the first. In an ironic twist, he secretly bought some of my work, realising its potential, and made money from dealing in the sale of that, too.

You lie there longing for the revitalising waters of the Mediterranean. In Turkey that time swimming off the little shingle beach. With her recuperating from one of her bouts of ill health. Waving at you from her towel by the shore, that sad and disconcerting stare from beneath her sunglasses. You knew it was there. That she was not cured. That she could never be cured. You spluttered along in your little pedalo, enchanted but alone. That crystalline sky, that salted sea, and that deep, throbbing heat couldn't medicate against her condition. In the evenings you drank Raki and wandered down to the marketplace where the old man, with the strong Turkish cigarettes, cooked the best burgers on the planet, over an open grill. They had all been there in the land of the crusaders, the Romans, the Greeks, the Phoenicians. The Byzantine empire that had stretched along her coast and the rattle and explosions of bullets and shells in those dramatic days in the Dardanelles. That warm sunshine and the drifting, exotic scent of burnished heat wafting over from the Middle East. Somewhere out there was a peripatetic journey to the Chinese shoreline of the Pacific ocean. Momentarily, you even considered trying it, to escape the confines of a difficult and cloying relationship. Who were you to tell your troubles to?

'How are you doing, Mum?'

'I'm fine, son. How are you? Sorry, we haven't spoken in a while.'

'No, it's okay, it's my fault. I've just been really busy, you know.'

'It's good to keep busy.'

'How's Dad?'

'Oh, you know, your father's your father.'

Why did I love you? Was it that your world seemed so perfect in a way, maybe just too perfect for you? Christmas at your home, your disarming parents and their effortless English middle class mannerisms, kisses and hugs for their returning children, holidays in the Dordogne, dinner parties and apéritifs. Two Labour-voting, home-counties English teachers, comfortable in their skin and the world they inhabited. Your sister and her boyfriend, both solicitors, appearing with Christmas gifts for all, including me, to be placed, with wrappings and bows, under the real Norwegian spruce in the dining room. Your brother phoning on Christmas morning from his gap year in New Zealand, which included a mumbled awkward conversation with me, hungover from too much wine on Christmas Eve. But your mother glanced at you, often, searching out the tell-tale signs that things were getting overwrought again. That the pills you discretely swallowed weren't working anymore. Your father seemed lost with you; tender, attentive, but ultimately unable to save his little girl. Your sister preferring the notion that things would always be the way they were that Christmas.

You wouldn't share another with them.

'Merry Christmas, everyone. God bless us, one and all,' your father toasts gregariously, already a little tipsy.

'Merry Christmas,' we all return fondly.

A fever-ridden corpse, tangled in the shroud of its own mortality. Freedom, a last gasp and whimper away. There would be no return journey, just an improbable emptiness. The very same state of existence for billions of years past and billions more years hence. Even the longest of lives is the briefest of flickers. Unnoticed and uncommented on by time itself. In space we are the merest specks, unobserved in the vastness of an expanding universe. He knows only what has been and what, truly, does he know of that?

We continued with the farce. The game must always be played out to the end. She phoned one Monday evening, inviting me round for some supper. She made that garlic, lemon and chilli chicken for the first and last time. It was one of those meals I understood immediately that I would remember forever. It was the most sensual moment in our brief relationship. Her mask was unveiled, she was sweet and homely: intimate. She spoke for the first time of her past, her true past, or as true as it would ever seem. Her sister's death in a skiing accident, when on vacation from Cambridge. They weren't close, they were too different for that. The sister, into hockey and horse-riding, both a runner and a rower. Daddy's girl, the sportsman he never had. She was flighty and fickle, a capricious and perennial daydreamer. The father was a surgeon, the mother a failed novelist. She wasn't especially close to either but excelled at drama at boarding school, where she existed in the shadow of her more popular and more beautiful sister. The grieving father lost himself in his beloved golf club, the mother in an eight-year affair that eventually resulted in remarriage after her father's fatal cardiac arrest at the nineteenth hole. It seems mother and daughter split the family silver straight down the middle and went their separate ways. Both independently wealthy, after a fashion. The mother still pined for her only surviving child. She seemed to be in a state of semi-permanent abandonment of all responsibility. Which I empathised with only too readily.

You tried something different with them all, but there was always something missing. There was a link in your existence that could not manifest itself. Why were you always so separate? Was it deliberate? Not long after the end of the relationship, your own sibling died in a tragic accident. Did you feel the empathy then? Was she as scarred by it as you?

Two close friends had vacated their home after the Christmas holidays and journeyed back to London. They invited me down in the new year as I made another lame attempt at straightening myself out. They ran a successful design business, had two small children, and were very much still in love. I enjoyed spending time with people who reminded me it was possible to have a life without sacrificing everything. They were confident individuals, secure in their relationship, environmentally committed and non-prejudiced. He had inherited a family home in Sandbanks in Poole, in which they took up residency during holidays in the off season and for two weeks in the summer, where they entertained their friends. The people they knew seemed so grown up, and so many of the people I knew seemed so lost.

They never judged you for your lifestyle, which you contrived not to judge them for. You were open with them and you asked nothing in return. You donated a couple of works to their house, *gratis*. You hoped one day the children could sell them for a fortune. It struck you as a sweet story. Years later, when they briefly became too ambitious, took some bad advice and over-extended their business, you invested some money in it. They never asked, you simply offered. You cared little for materialistic wealth, but you wanted them to succeed. You wanted to believe in that life, that it was possible. You remained committed to them always and they continued to be resolutely loyal to you.

I trawled through that house, judging the photographs, curious of the personal history which had passed through it. Could I ever have owned such a place? Filled with so many memories. I sketched, fasted, paced the beach, watched the tide turn four times a day for a whole month. It wasn't one of the super-deluxe houses being built, but it had character and charm. Not some gaudy genuflection at the foot of mammon for the wealthy; people I knew only too well and detested readily. The house had, at one point in time, been a genuine home, and it kept a sense of that within its walls.

Petrified in your maudlin shell, your paranoia, self-abatement and lacerations against the world ran on, unchecked. You secreted sweat on the sheets at night and shivered recklessly through the new dawn breaking over the English Channel. Another year and less the wiser. Your brain semi-permanently unfocused. You sketched the waves in rhythms of monotonal variations and etched in pencil the undulations of the grey sea and the dark sky. You drew to live. You created to survive. It was all you knew. It was all you had known. It was all you would ever know.

The sails flap in the wind. A leisurely breeze ripples the waves along the shore. I ride along in the stern of the ship. They are at the helm, steering a course through the blue, tranquil sea in a loving embrace. I push my hand through the cold, murky water. It is twilight. I pull a matted clump of seaweed from the froth. It is the hair of my brother. I immediately drop him back into the depths of blackness below. A sinking emotion clings to my heart and I begin to weep. A strange stirring of home sickness is replaced with a maudlin dread. I think only of death.

The wounded heart of the nocturne has been pierced and the solar light will make its daily revolution once more. In the sky, towards the east, there are glimmerings of luminance. It has not yet arrived: the light that will bring life to the earth and contain humanity within its rays.

Why did I come to this place, here? An exotic dénouement to my journey, in a land of wilderness I do not recognise, amongst a people I have never encountered. What do they make of this stranger among them? This abandoned invalid from a land overseas, who they have carried to his grave.

Her games continued on. She had procured, from a costumers, a dandified squire's outfit for me to wear. She was regaled in the garments of a village wench from the local inn and beseeched me to have my wicked way with her, however I fancied. I tied her gently to the bedposts using her own silk scarfs and ravaged her until we had had our fill. She played the role of dominant and submissive with equal ease and grace. I was less convinced with my part, but played along all the same. I was perhaps too gentle a soul for her tastes, but I always had the feeling she liked me deeply all the same. If we had only registered the proper emotions and feelings for each other, we may have expressed them better.

The studio had started to feel like a curse, it was littered with empty bottles and little in the way of new artworks. There were magazines and newspapers scattered around and some catalogues from an exhibition. It was cold and gloomy in the pale winter light. In the corner was a desk with a seldom-used computer. For the first time in my artistic career I began to plan drawings by describing them in text before transferring them to a visual language. I never completed any of them.

You were disgusted by your tools: disgusted with yourself. To complete a line was to commit. You were incapable of such an act. You could not free yourself from the fear that your career had ended already. Resigned to the indignity of obscurity, your work would fade then erode into dust. Nobody would be able to recount your oeuvre, what it may have meant, or have been able to place it within the confines of a cultural relic, from a specified period.

Standing in a room of the Museo del Prado with you, entranced by Goya's late, black paintings. You could only witness mental illness and I could only imagine genius. A personal incapability to comprehend what it takes to be that great. To translate the plasticity of paint into such carnivorous images of despair. I walked through them all in the trauma of a nightmare. The world in the eyes of a man so much more capable than others. A man far beyond the realms of any talent which I possessed.

If I look and see it now, your hallowed, beatific face, in amongst the crowds, your hand scribbling away furiously in the leather-bound pad you carried everywhere with you. Your blonde hair held up; your peach-fresh complexion; your pink, sensuous lips: the prettiest angel in Madrid. I must have loved you then, crazy to walk hand-in-hand with you, to a café, for the hot chocolate and churros you enjoyed so much. How dreadful we can't predict the future, how dreadful and how marvellous.

Hungover and generally out of sorts, lounging on the sofa, the phone rang in the studio and I was invited to dinner. You presented a wonderful bowl of Spaghetti Bolognese; cooked lovingly for a couple of hours, the meat was tender, the sauce unctuous, dressed with a pungent dose of flat-leaf parsley and parmesan cheese, it was a hearty mix of maximum umami. I remember that meal so vividly; it was our last supper together. We drank a decent bottle of Barolo together, from crystal wine glasses, before retreating to the lounge.

'I've got something special for us to try. A little treat.' Those are the last words I recall you ever saying.

You coyly produced a silver dessert spoon and a hollow stainless steel tube. From a small paper wrap, you produced a dusty brown powder and carefully sprinkled it on the spoon. You took a cheap red plastic lighter, placed it directly underneath the spoon and melted the powder into a liquid. You sucked a long drawl of the fumes and held them down. You passed the tube to me and offered the spoon. I drew in the chemically acrid, contaminated air. I immediately vomited into a small wastepaper bin close by. You showed no displeasure at the action and we continued on. I remember the pain evaporating. I remember everything evaporating, folding in upon itself, until only the reality of unreality was real anymore.

We come scrambling out of the womb and go screaming back into the tomb. The places and spaces in between are our salvation and our purgatory. The doors of this world are left ajar and invite us in, some we accept and some we decline. I stumbled into your world and you into mine. We passed each other briefly, over the course of ten months, or a year. When we came back from our sojourn in an opium dream we were sick and changed.

You spent two days in a post-morphine haze, in a lonely double bed, cowed in white linen sheets, in a room devoid of any other furniture, in your small South London flat. The doorbell rang and you thought it was the drug squad come to raid you, or a collector come to murder you for supplying them with a dodgy knock-off artwork. You sweated and grimaced, panted and groaned and tried to retch but had no solids to give. The high was a high and the low was a low.

The brown stained walls are heaving and pulsing, a red womb is pumping noxious gasses around your body. The clouded vapour wisps its way through the corridors of the bloodied flesh surrounding you. Stripped carcasses of strange hybrid animals abound. Inside a hollowed-out human foot is a pool of wine. You touch the skin and it fuses to your hand. You cannot rid yourself of the foot. The wine splashes into a pool of muddy water and you submerge yourself in it. She swims towards you with her penis erect. She closes your eyes and the organic enclosure begins to pound and wail.

We never met again. She departed for the States and a part in an off-Broadway play. Time and distance suspended between our two worlds: between our two lives. A trajectory which touched for the briefest of instants before fading once more into a cosmic nothingness. What became of either of us, I could never know.

The herdsmen shall sleep on. An entire people shall sleep on, until the all-consuming light of the coming dawn. The livestock will shelter and rest while the night remains still. In the whispering air, the grains of sand will whip themselves abrasively against one another, part company, rise and fall again.

My brother is dead, the sea killed him. His body tossed in great waves, his arms grasping helplessly at the froth. His head sinking beneath the waterline, his lungs glugging down their last of the great North Sea's salty brine. A bloated corpse sinking towards Norway.

I spent over a month camped in the studio, hardly resting, surviving on nuts and dried fruit, bottled water and vitamin pills. I worked day and night, dusk till dawn, to complete fifteen abstract works on paper and canvas which I titled: *The Death Series*. The negation of all, drawn up in pigment of the deepest black; a raven black, with the darkest of reds mixed in. Geometric and biomorphic forms and shapes, entering and leaving one another, interacting and separating, solidity and dissolution, extraction and refraction. Feeding my way through compositions unopposed by intellectual designs, riven by a sense of grief, morbidity, maudlin rancour, confusion and disbelief. My brother was dead. That part of me, that was connected with this other to the host womb, to biology and genetics. So different from me, so aggressive towards me, so grievous in his caustic approach to me; so senseless his being, so tragic his death.

In some strange way, the work was my eulogy for my brother, to mark the passing of a kind of primal attachment I couldn't share with any other. We two were built of the same genetic codes, implanted by our parents and their ancestors before them.

The gallerists, dealers and collectors come out of their coffins when they smell money or a profit. *The Death Series* was hung and a new kind of fiend crawled out of the shadows: curators. There were the ubiquitous prints and book, newspaper and magazine articles. Nothing sells like misery. I displayed my expected public outpouring of grief and despair, guilt and disillusionment over my brother's death, even though we hadn't been in close contact for a number of years before his untimely demise. They wrote the pieces up with abandonment and without missing a glibly rendered cliché. A gallery in Utrecht wished to display the works and eagerly courted my assistance in displaying the pieces. I don't know if I was much help. I spent most of the time in Amsterdam, smoking skunk in hash bars. Existing on a diet of Dutch beer, coffee, tortilla chips, bread and chocolate spread. I played bar football with the locals and stared at prostitutes in windows, curious if I would see you, in a new guise. I pined for your body still and your unnerving sense of pure libertinism. After you, everything felt so stale. I took a bad trip in a seedy hotel with a red light flashing constantly in through the window. I didn't leave the room for two days and just barely made it to the opening of my own first exhibition in the Netherlands.

I lie in the bed, old worn blankets curled around me. The furniture is ancient pre-war stuff. In the mirror is a German officer in a black SS uniform. His pistol is drawn. From underneath the mattress you pull out a revolver and spring from the bed. You both shoot one another but neither is injured. I am walking down the corridor of an old factory. A man turns towards me and says, 'They are burning people, turning them into smoke.' I look in a large room in which people are sitting around an open fire, puffing on a hookah placed in the centre of it. The air is foggy. Smoke fills my lungs and brings on a coughing fit. You stand staring at the black blood you have spat out on the freshly polished tiles.

I was haggard in a newly-bought black designer suit, white shirt and skinny black tie: the *apparel de jour*. I caught a glimpse of the prettiest girl in the gallery. Your blonde hair held up, your tight black leather jacket and your short white dress. You were deeply enthralled in conversation with an older woman, an as yet untouched wine glass in your hand. I observed you as you gathered in front of each picture and were then pointed towards the artist: me. I swaggered to you and you smiled coyly. Two glasses of cheap red wine had confused me. I hadn't eaten all day and was cerebrally mashed from my Dutch drug orgy. I shook your firm, dry hand; petite and like your face, blemish-free. There was a wholesome, kharmic centre to you, so at odds with my hell-bound hide. My head felt muddy and bleached out and you appeared as an apparition of goodness opposing the evil in my soul. You softly stated your name and I instantly forgot it. I excused myself and went outside to the humid continental summer air. I swallowed down some painkillers with champagne and retched a little. The sweat stuck the shirt to my back and I loosened the tie as best as I could. I wondered if I would collapse right there and decease on the spot. You took my arm and asked if I was doing fine. I turned and you were gone. Were you ever there? You had left the gallery, but not my life. I would locate you again in Amsterdam, writing a paper on a female painter resident in Holland.

In the dark, the universe sucks all light matter from the world. It swallows it whole and regurgitates it up in the farthest constellations in the heavens. It mocks and taunts the trembling human soul, devoid of luminance and hope. The blackness devours all spatial contours and mental connection with physical life.

I searched for you. I asked around the Dutch cultural community until I pinpointed you at a small, cheap hotel by a canal. With an all-consuming arrogance I walked into a café and seated myself beside you. Eventually, you glanced up from your book, but kept on writing in your pad. I inquired as to your opinion on my exhibition. You considered it a necessary detour in my career. A moving, if grief-drenched, weigh station. A respite to cleanse my palette, before continuing on with my own irrepressible and iconoclastic voice. I complimented you on your gorgeous green eyes and asked if I could buy an impoverished scholar a proper meal with metal cutlery and everything. You held me in the suspicion of an academic who doesn't want to get too close to their subject, even though you were actually completing a Ph.D in post-colonial female artists at Goldsmiths. You had already obtained your degree from Cambridge and an MA from the Royal College of Art, where you still did some teaching. Your credentials were impeccable but I had, during the course of my career, met more impressive CVs. It wasn't a sticking point and neither was your relative youth at twenty-four years of age. I was most impressed with your beauty and your unmistakable way of avoiding it at all costs. You seemed genuinely indifferent to it, which I found to be highly original. When, later in our relationship, I viewed portraits of former boyfriends, I was less convinced. One literally paid his way through university by modelling. You had never dated an artist: you had yet to meet your Picasso.

Six months later you were living in a two-bedroom apartment in the Barbican with her. You moved your studio back north of the river to a semi-derelict space in Hoxton. The art world was ablaze with shows everywhere. You and she went to them all. Stood among the culturally elect: the new arbiters of taste. You were no longer an arriviste but a fully-fledged member of the cultural cognoscenti: the elite. With that badge of honour went respect, ingratiation and sycophancy. You adapted to it all. You two became an indispensable item, to be photographed smoochingly at every after-show party. You, with your artistic pedigree; her, with her academic credentials. The perfect symbiosis of God-given talent and hard-won intellectual superiority. She never acted upon it and neither did you.

It took living with her to realise not everything was okay in her world. She took pills to maintain an equilibrium in the state of her mental health.

There were good days, there were bad days, and there were monstrous days. I was to become party to them all, the ups and downs, the ebbs and flows, the hyper-volatility and the partial psychosis. I had never, ever witnessed another human being cry so hard and for so long as her, opening up entirely with neither warning nor explanation. The first time, it left me in shock. The second, it broke my heart.

'I feel so terrible. I just want to die.' She trembles, her face a damp mass of tears.

'I know, I know. It'll be okay, it'll pass,' I offer hopelessly.

I could do nothing, I was terminally impotent as to her condition. The doctors swapped pills, changed doses, did what little they could. She was terrified of being committed to a mental institution and paranoid in the extreme that she would receive electroconvulsive therapy treatment. I promised her I would never allow it. I have little idea now and had none at the time how exactly I was going to extricate her from such a situation. I still felt it was my duty to attempt it, however futile it might prove to be. I said we would flee the country and live abroad. She said that would condemn her career to ruin and possibly damage mine, too. I told her, for me, she was worth it. I would keep creating. I would always create. It would be our salvation. It could never have saved her from a fate that now seems to have been an inevitable part of her condition. Illness so easily breaks the will and it eventually broke mine. I sought solace more and more in alcohol and drugs and a discrete affair with the young barmaid in a pub around the corner from my studio. With her,

I rekindled my good spirits and humour, but there was always that moment when it was time to return home again.

'What is it you do here?' she asks, taking another hit on the joint.

'Draw and paint, sometimes. A lot of the time I do nothing at all,' I answer, nonplussed.

'And you can earn a living from that?'

'It depends on the circumstances. How good you are. Whether or not you have a gallery behind you. That kind of thing.'

'Does she paint?'

'Who?'

'Your girlfriend.' She looks at me slyly. I have never discussed being in a relationship with another woman.

At which point do we choose our lives? Do we essentially remain children, with the world simply thrust at us in a relentless cascade towards our inevitable oblivion? I feel I never lived, but merely existed. I was frozen inside of a vacuum, not of my making but willed on to me by some ambivalent force of evolution. I could not step out of myself, escape from my own being: avoid my nature. Is this the curse of all humans? Are we eternally condemned to exist as us and us alone?

Nobody helped you. Nobody could advise you as to the best course of action to take. You remained loyal to her, even though you increasingly extricated yourself from the relationship. Were you what she needed? In your own timely way, you abandoned her. You didn't envisage the end as it came, but it always held precedence in your thoughts. She was young, she was beautiful, she was intelligent, she was gifted, she was cursed. Did it matter in the end that you had once loved her?

He groans outwardly from beneath the soiled sheet. It does not penetrate the silence compressing the room into a volumeless chasm. He is unmistakably alone, in a drifting mass of nothingness floating through a pitch-black, bottomless void. His hand strains to tether itself onto a physical reality. His ears strain to gather a merest murmur of sound. His eyes are too weak to venture into the meekest of light. His lungs cling to the airless room, searching for breath.

I was commissioned for a show in New York, in a newly opened SoHo gallery. I was free to conceive of my own work. It was the beginning of a series of contemporary masters, at least that's how they sold it. My exhibition slipped in between shows by a female video and performance artist and a newly-emerging immersive sculptor. The gallery had set itself an exhaustive précis of the insurgent bull market for art collecting.

So began my monumental undertaking for a continuing series entitled: *Heroes*. In so many ways, my artistic magnum opus. I spent several weeks trawling all corners of the five boroughs of New York City: shops, cafés, diners, restaurants, bars, parks, the beach, cinemas, theatres; collecting sketches for the final, completed work. I filled sketch pad after sketch pad and took reams of film with my trusted Leica. It took three weeks of solid work to complete the images on the gallery walls, rendered in paint, pastel, chalk, ink, charcoal and graphite. The piece encompassed many legendary and famous people from African American culture: Martin Luther King, Malcolm X, Marcus Garvey, Booker T Washington, Rosa Parks, Jesse Jackson, Bessie Smith, Nina Simone, Ella Fitzgerald, Billie Holliday, Louis Armstrong, Miles Davis, John Coltrane, BB King, Sidney Poitier, Jesse Owens, Muhammed Ali, Richard Pryor, Eddie Murphy, Ice Cube, Ice T, Diana Ross, Michael Jackson, Marvin Gaye, Huey Newton, Stokely Carmichael, Jimi Hendrix, Maya Angelou, Oprah Winfrey, Michael Jordan, Magic Johnson, Jean-Michel Basquiat, James Baldwin, Scott Joplin, Grandmaster Flash, Gordon Parks, Toni Morrison, Spike Lee, Denzel Washington, Samuel L Jackson, Harry Belafonte, Pam Grier, Stevie Wonder, Nat King Cole,

Sammy Davis Junior, Chuck D, Dr Dre, Flavor Flav, James Earl Jones, Josephine Baker, W. E. B. Du Bois, Aretha Franklin, Tina Turner, Yaphet Kotto, Tracy Chapman, Wilson Pickett, Red Foxx, Muddy Waters, Alex Haley and Rodney King. The images of these famous individuals shimmered on the white walls and magnified in and out of focus. The portraits themselves were made up of the drawings I produced of the ordinary black people I witnessed on the streets of New York. It was the imagery of an entire cultural machine backed up by, and in some ways representative of, a whole section of society. While still questioning who really speaks for us and if they are always necessarily democratically chosen to do so on our behalf. The show caused a sensation within the New York art world, before sending ripples out into the hinterland. Who was I, a white British person, to represent black American culture? Where were all the individuals that were missing? Why wasn't a black American artist allowed to exhibit instead of me? Why was American culture and politics underrepresented by African Americans? Where were the Hispanic American heroes? Where were the Native American heroes? Where were all the Italian American heroes? Where were all the white American heroes? There were calls of boycott from the black community, the white community, and the Irish American community. I was castigated by one white female commentator for reducing black American history down to mere cultural signifiers. There were cues around the block, every day, of people waiting to view the exhibition. The show was a sell-out and ran for six weeks from September into the deep Fall, before transferring in a reduced form to LA in the new year. I was interviewed by newspapers, magazines, television and radio shows. I was asked: *why this exhibition?* and simply retorted that I had witnessed a young woman beaten to death by a police officer. To all the criticism, I countered that my biography could not exist without the interference of African American culture, from the *Roots* TV programme through

Eddie Murphy being the coolest person on the planet in the early Eighties, to every genre of music I listened to. Black America was always present and correct.

'But why just black America? Why not simply America as a whole?'

'Why no Thomas Jefferson?'

'Why no Abraham Lincoln?'

'Why is African American history representative of the biography of a white guy from the Highlands of Scotland?'

'Why didn't you complete a cultural survey of your own country? Your own people?'

'Are you ashamed of Scotland?'

'Are you uninterested in the cultural and political life of black British people?'

She was there with you, supplying the best lines, the rationale, mounting your defence. You could never get past the art; the reason for its creation was within you, not exterior in the body cultural that existed permanently around you. You were its sole progenitor, you and you alone. You could never answer otherwise. You were fêted everywhere. The artist and his intellectual and beautiful muse. The darling art world couple in Manhattan: the little Britishers. It could never have lasted for her, some biographies are just too good.

It was difficult being back home. All the energy, inspiration and perspiration had evaporated. London never did have the razzmatazz and pizzazz that New York could produce in the toss of a dime. It was an empty, blank period, which appeared to exacerbate your condition. Christmas at your parents' gave some light relief before a late January schlep to the Sunshine State. I didn't possess the necessary enthusiasm or stamina for a tooled-down and rebooted version of the New York show in LA. Art always felt like a mere backdrop to the entertainments industry there; a poorer second cousin, patronisingly showered with unwanted, unnecessary gifts. But my relationship with my gallery there was paramount to my career. I sensed and understood it and you hammered the equation home. You knew the art world; comprehended it, felt its vitality as an electrical connection running through the core of your being. You were interested in nothing else.

'That gallery's on the up. You're in on the ground floor. They're looking to take dominion over the global market. The gallery at home's small change in comparison with them. They're going to be a behemoth. You've got to see past LA and look at the wider strategic picture; pardon the pun. They're ambitious and they're serious. You've got to match that. You're a great artist, but you have to prove it time and time again for the art world to take note, sit up and listen properly.'

Life culls the weak and death scythes the weak and strong alike. So many people were envious of you: the beauty; the intelligence; your sweet, positive nature; the steely determination with which you tackled everything; your quiet wit; the artist boyfriend; your qualifications; your career; the opportunities afforded you, and the brilliant future which so obviously lay ahead. None of it meant anything. You killed yourself anyway. In spite of everything, nothing could have prevented it. Were you too greedy for life, or was it too greedy for you? Whatever else I was, I wasn't able to hold on to you; nobody was. I couldn't have prevented any of it and I never tried.

My parents wrestled themselves from their native land and sojourned to London in the early summer. I offered to put them up in the flat in the Barbican, but they insisted on staying in a modest hotel in Pimlico instead. I offered to recompense them for their outlay, but they wouldn't hear of that, either. My father enjoyed the old masters in the National Gallery, my mother enjoyed afternoon tea at Claridge's, and they were both as giddy as schoolchildren on the open-topped bus tour around the capital's famous sites.

'It's somehow smaller than I thought it would be. I mean the buildings and the streets and stuff. Of course, it's far more grand than we're used to at home,' my mother tells you in a pizza joint after two pinot grigios.

'You can see why it was at the heart of an empire,' my father effuses. 'It's all so grand.'

'We saw the Houses of Parliament. It's so funny seeing it for real after all these years of seeing it on the telly,' my mother continues, warming to her subject. 'And Buckingham Palace, now that was grand. Is the Queen in residence when the flag's flying, I can't remember? I've had too much wine. It's been a tiring day.'

I thought for a time they might forget their collective pain and grief at my brother's passing. Whatever their feelings, they kept them in reserve. I attempted to charm them all the same, even though I was ill at the time. I attempted to play the gracious host and dutiful son, but I too was exhausted from producing the recent exhibitions in the States. They seemed aged to me, especially my father. He had always appeared to me slightly aloof and sad, though he had a great propensity for laughter also. My mother was unnerved by the giant metropolis at first, but seemed to relax into it all by the end. I'm not sure either of them really wished to return home. Perhaps they didn't want to return to each other, to an unspeakable heartbreak which was tearing them apart. What now should I have done? How should I have responded otherwise? I kissed her, shook his hand, and never saw them again. How odd now that it should have all felt so natural. Families ripped away from each other in wars and migrations, and we waved each other a pleasant goodbye on the train platform at Euston Station.

My father was born and raised in Glasgow in comfortably working-class surroundings. My grandfather was a carpenter who had fought in the Second World War and could perhaps have helped liberate Belsen. My father was always unclear on the matter. My grandfather never, ever spoke of it. He always appeared to me distant and a little severe, but I also remember him as generous and protective of my brother and I. On holiday, he would take us to a pond with rowing boats and buy us chips and '99' ice creams with hundreds and thousands scattered on top. I can still recall big department stores with escalators. My grandmother's homemade steak pie with mashed potatoes and mushy peas. The guilty feeling because I liked my grandmother's cooking better than my mother's. My father's sister married and moved to Newcastle. It was she who bought me my first drawing book.

I wonder if my father had liked to draw, also. He moved to the Highlands and became a labourer. I think that always disappointed his father, as he was a tradesman. The only possible ambition my father ever revealed to me was that he had a notion to become a chef when he left school. My grandfather dissuaded him, due to the long, unsociable hours and the uninspiring nature of the job. So he took a job with a construction firm, with a contract to build new social housing up north, and never returned to live in Glasgow again.

My mother had worked as a chambermaid in a local hotel when we were kids; for some pin money, I suppose, and for when my father was between jobs. When we were older she worked in a café, then a local supermarket, followed by a traditional clothing shop. She had started out her working life in the laundry of the hospital. She had dreamed of being a nurse but never had the courage, nor the conviction, to follow through on it. She always maintained the highest regard for people in health professions, throughout her entire life. She was an only child of elderly parents. Her father was already forty-two when she was born and he died of emphysema when she was just five. My mother gave off the impression that she had always been old, as though her childhood had never existed. It was spent with a work-worn, melancholic widow. It was all frugality and rations, early nights and endless chores. She always seemed to approach life like she was standing on the sidelines, never entirely taking part in it all. Was that what she and my father saw in the other? They had parenthood to bond them, then grief, and then dislocation.

A sublime kind of silence forms in the night in the desert. A penetrating darkness pierced only by the generous moonlight. Luminance enough to make someone more aware of the dangers which lurk in the shadows beyond the liminal space which the eyes can scour. The herdsmen, unsettled, keep tender watch over their cattle and into the surrounding wasteland of dust and sand and scrub.

That solipsism that has stalked me all of my life, from childhood to this silent sarcophagus at the edge of the world. From pine forests and glens to whipping winds and desert sands, it has fallen upon me to chart the course of my own existence.

How calm it was without you. The guilt flashed through my heart thirty times a minute. The bed clothing, the quilt, the pillows all incinerated. The bed, the mattress, remained, along with that spirit of death and decay. It never flushed itself fully of that feeling: the memory was always retained.

You punished yourself with it. You had let her fall into her grave. You had let your brother die and later your parents, too. There was you and you alone in life. Your mission had to be completed, whatever the cost to others or yourself. It was demanded of you as an artist. You only had one fleeting lunge at grasping immortality. You were born gifted, though you never entirely rejoiced in it.

It is difficult to appease the gods, they demand so much of us. On the sacrificial pyre was my tragic love affair, which the art world mourned as a dutiful parasite sucking all life from your biography. Layering the details of provenance, the insights, the critique, the mystique, the immersive subconscious. It would aid the scripting of catalogues, articles, papers, gilding the lily. And so I was met with doleful eyes, searching looks, words of comfort and sympathy. Would I follow her into the tomb? The prices of my work edged up a little.

The studio was suddenly more inviting, though little enough took place there. I would sit in the evenings, wrapped in an Afghan blanket, coddling bottles of continental beers, staring at the blank walls, drifting in and out of wakefulness. My mind blanked off from reality as people around me pedalled and pushed their way to work and pleasure. I discovered a timelessly authentic greasy spoon around the corner, in which every day around noon I would devour a full English breakfast with chips and bread and butter, all washed down with cups of hot, sticky tea. It was my only sustenance for the day. The apartment in the Barbican grew dusty and musky from the absence of human lifeforms. I eventually hired a cleaner to spruce it up twice a week. It must have been the easiest money she ever made. I threw her bonuses anyway, in respect of my heritage. My days were gripped by an evangelical listlessness. I began a drawing of a flower in a jar of water, then ceased almost immediately. I filled sketchbooks with partially-completed red roses, finishing with a fully realised sketch of a decayed, petal-less stem. I went back and tinted the flowers with ink then pressed the head of one rose inside each sketchbook, before filing them away forever. I suppose they must have been some kind of botanical rendering of grief. I dismissed it as a type of bored impatience at the time. I never bore witness to them again.

Terror grips the soul of the artist who wishes to create and cannot. The crushing quest for truth, for originality and authenticity, triumph over all other considerations. The night is dark and the day is dull without the will and power to bring new form into the world. There is an empty vacuum at the heart of everything, whose space can only be colonised by the creation of new work. Despair must never be allowed to take root and expand its carcinogenic outpourings into the consciousness of the artist. With fear of failure comes a deeper knowledge and exploration of this phenomenon as the default state of all art: it is all damned to failure.

I missed you with a greater depth than I would acknowledge. It wasn't all based on that grim reaper called guilt. With your death came an intense solitude: the discussions, the arguments, the passion, the moments of drama, were all erased immediately, without warning. People avoided me more, afraid that the taint of mortality might contaminate them too, as though death was contagious. The once-golden couple had taken on the patina of misfortune. It dripped off my being and poisoned the ether surrounding everybody. People positioned within the art world were young, hip, cool, successful, wealthy, powerful, and they wanted to remain that way; nobody wished to be deceased. They all wanted to deny it, of themselves and of you. Even the journalists seemed to stop calling.

I was invited to take part in a group exhibition in London titled: *Fin de Siècle*. I forced myself to awake in the studio every morning and work. For the first week I did little of anything; drank red wine, smoked weed and dabbled a little with speed, which didn't do anything at all for my creative instincts. I witnessed you again, each and every night, more decayed than the last. The worms and maggots crawling through the mattress to devour your skin and the flesh beneath it. I felt I would go mad. By the second week I was on vodka, Valium and sleeping pills. All of which did nothing for anything, except to bring me closer to your mortal state. On the third week I went home to the flat, got into bed, and stayed there for five days of cold, hard turkey.

You stand beatific before me, pleadingly holding out your hands. Your wrists open and solidified red paint streams towards me. We kiss passionately, but you are her and she is not you. Your mother sits in the corner of the studio watching television. Your father is at the table, reading. You whisper, 'I'm not here,' or do you say, 'I'm not her'? You are standing before me, dressed as you were that first day we met, trembling and weeping. 'I'm not well,' you say. He stands there comforting you, but it is no longer you, it is someone else, but it is you. 'I've got a drawing for you,' he says. He goes to a drawer in their hotel bedroom. He takes out a charcoal drawing of Saint Paul's Cathedral. 'Look, it's the church I used to go to,' I say. 'I don't go to church,' she says, confused. She then looks around the apartment's kitchen and says, 'Did I drink all the wine?'

'I'm going to bed now,' she concludes, and wraps herself in a white sheet on a sofa in her childhood home. Your breath sucks the white sheet into a hollow and it begins to stain brown.

I shivered and shook, vomited a few times, sweated profusely, shit the bed once, drowned vitamin pills with fruit juices, smoothie concoctions of carrots and avocados, limes, lemons, grapefruits, tomatoes, strawberries and mango. I ate salads and posh soups brought to me by the cleaner, who gallantly washed the sheets, and quit her job ten days later. On the fifth week I returned to the studio, cleaned the place out, and settled down to work.

I drew, by necessity, you. I reasoned you would have acquiesced to such an ardent request. The shocking beauty I remembered in your state of repose, with the sick congealed to the side of your face. That strange expression freeze-framed in your eyes, as though you were so relieved to be done with it all. I produced composition after composition until that look was proficiently realised. Then came the other drawings: a product of my nightmares. Your corpse sinking and collapsing in on itself in a spore-like mass of dense charcoal, graphite and ink. The decomposition of the body, intense and horrifyingly visceral. How I imagined your body to then be, enclosed within a wooden prison, under six feet of earth.

Does art cure us of our demons? They sit well with me still, unappeased by any exhortations and incantations I have ever sent to remedy them.

The gallery was ecstatic, you had played your hand so well. It was everything they and the public demanded and desired. A holy trinity, of mortality, grief, and controversy. Sealed and guaranteed to have commentators talking, reactionaries flapping, and the press providing free advertisement. You didn't hang around for the plaudits and the scourgings. The art works were completed, the sales were made, and the payments received. You fled to the relative safety and anonymity of County Cork in Ireland and a small cottage by Bantry Bay.

They fester within you - success and failure - with equal tenacity. I sat hypnotised by the peat flames in the hearth, sipping some Irish whiskey, which I claimed to the locals was inferior to the real water of life from the Highlands and Islands of Alba. We laughed and chatted over a few pints of Guinness in an authentic Irish bar in Bantry Town. Mostly, I wandered through the countryside and by the shoreline of the bay. There was never a place I ever saw that was as green as Ireland. Though other parts of the hinterland reminded me of my own Celtic homeland. For a moment I even considered a trip back to the old country, but it never materialised into anything concrete. Would it have brought any comfort to my parents or me? The theory was never tested.

In the dusty plains, the wildlife is ravenous, scavenging for any morsel of food and asylum from harsh winds and cruel sunlight. In the darkened room, insects fester around his dying body. A brief movement beneath his death shroud sends some scuttling, but more still are inspired. Where there is life there is sustenance. Where there is sickness there are rich, easy pickings. They all hover ghoulishly above him in some macabre dance of death. He will expire and succumb to the lifeless form he is destined to be. His usefulness on earth will not end there, for then he shall become nutrients for the living.

I always felt the gloom of London, whenever I returned. In the quiet and peace of the countryside your thoughts are calm and wise. The city doesn't trade in sagacity, it deals in trauma, neurosis and chaos. Adversity is a state of mind, it supplants weakness with strength, failure with success.

Though it is never a scientific transaction. It can so often, and so easily does, turn triumph into defeat. The city is the perfect psychological projection of the human being, in all of its myriad forms. It is mean, squat, ugly, avaricious, licentious, prurient, caustic, charismatic, enigmatic, corrupt, voluptuous, sensuous, bilious, prudish, censorious, liberal, libertine, gregarious, solicitous, benevolent, malevolent, beautiful, magnificent, and downright evil. Its dictatorial project reigns supremely over all other matter on earth. Only at these instants of reignited contact is it possible to divine any of this as, soon enough, the individual ferments once again in the belly of the beast and then all reason rapidly evaporates into its choleric fumes.

I had the drudgery of work to keep me involuntarily sane. There were a few magazine articles to facilitate, two catalogues to cast my eyes over, and a serious monograph of my work being produced by an academic. The latter rapidly grew into a major ball-ache. I was asked searching question after probing enquiry for hours on end.

'But it was an image-rich childhood, was it not? All those mountains and rivers and glens and lochs. I've been to the Highlands and it's quite stunning. One of the most extraordinary landscapes in the world. Then there was television, cinema, religious iconography designed to import the image as epiphany. It was a smorgasbord of visual delights, I imagine,' he says breathlessly.

'I don't know,' I reply exhaustedly.

I doubted anyone could work in such a detailed and meticulous manner as this man. It didn't seem possible without your head imploding first. He marvelled over the exegesis of his own text. Argued with me as to what I meant by a work. He employed philosophers, psychologists, writers, artists, and historical artefacts I had never in my life heard of. He made me despise my own art to the extent that I thought I would never create again. Finally, the purgatory of this pedant came to an end and I got drunk solidly for two whole days.

It had finally dawned upon you that London was changing, the world was expanding rapidly; exponentially faster every moment. Your youth had ended and you hadn't even witnessed its requiem. The elasticity of time stretches and contracts in a capricious and contrary accoutrement to our lives, as though it exists on its own plane, separate to the rhythms of our own biography. Your friends and acquaintances matured and developed without your consent. Their careers took off or ended; they got married; had children; fell in and out of love; moved galleries; swapped professions; bought houses in the country and holiday homes by the sea; went bankrupt; bought cars and apartments; emigrated. One died in a rock-climbing accident, one got cancer, and another wound up in a mental hospital. They got fat and they got thin; fell into drugs and fell out of them again; got rich and got poor; became famous and faded into obscurity once more. There was no particular pattern to frame any of it within a definitive, all-encompassing theory. You were at a loss to find a rationality for it all. Your life had escaped you; slipped through your fingers while you were engaged elsewhere. The once-thronging bars felt empty and lonely. They were all new faces, a different generation: a different era. You felt suddenly old, tired and defeated. It had been such a torturous ascent, so many gullies and crevices to lose your footing on. You ached and you fell sick, a type of existential illness; seemingly terminal and incurable.

That city brimming full of millions of people felt so empty all of a sudden. As though my eyes had just newly opened to find strangers everywhere. I stopped going to shows, even as the invitations multiplied. They felt strange and awkward without you. I sat in the apartment and watched television, cooked pasta and rice dishes and the occasional stir-fry with noodles. You had taught me how to cook them. I sipped dry white wines and ate bowls of mixed nuts and listened endlessly to hip hop and rap; so beloved by you and loathed by me.

I fell asleep often in the Eames recliner and awoke confused and staring out at the bright lights of old London Town. I stopped shaving for a while and put on a little weight around my midriff. I occasionally phoned my parents, concerned about their health and welfare. They had looked old to me, that last time we met; much older than they should have.

Was I merely drifting then, coasting my way into my middle years? It could have been so easy, so comfortable, to just pass on it all. I had strived so hard and for so long, and for what? To not become my parents? To escape from my humble background? Why do any of those things? Art was the only truth I had ever really known in life. It was a loyal, if wayward, companion. I only wished to prove to art how great I could be.

In the spring, I received a random and obscure request to create a site-specific artwork for a gallery in Tokyo. The owner of the gallery was a man I had been introduced to in LA. Only I couldn't remember him, who he was, or what he looked like. An apartment would be made available for me and guests during the summer and I would be given an entire room within the gallery with three ten-foot walls to play with. In the absence of any better offers, I immediately accepted the challenge and moved back to the studio full-time, abandoning the duplex in the Barbican, in this instance *sans* cleaner. I immediately intuited that the one-piece, three-wall artwork would be titled: *Who is Japan?* This was my personal prompt to create the piece around this specific endeavour. I made several trips along Charing Cross Road and began to collect books on Japanese culture. I watched films by Ozu and Kurusawa and Mizoguchi, and read novels by Kenzaburo Oe and Haruki Murakami. I read some Manga comics and watched a few Anime films. I discovered the television show *Monkey* was actually Japanese and not Chinese as I had, in my youth, initially thought. I watched documentaries on the Second World War. I bought history books which, in fairness, I never really got around to reading. For the most part I hoodwinked and blagged my way into the Japanese realm. I stopped drinking, I stopped taking drugs, I consumed healthy bean wraps, fruit juices, and lots of sushi. I began running a few K every morning, to get fit and to stay focused. I'm uncertain that any of it made any difference. In the end I went to Tokyo anyway. The city was in the midst of a summer heatwave and the humidity was utterly unbearable. I avoided the streets during the day and stayed inside my air-conditioned apartment and the equally air-controlled gallery which was close by. Every time I stepped outside the apartment block, I needed another shower. The sun, when it shone, was a burning furnace, and the rest of the time it rained, which merely added to the already unfeasibly dense atmosphere. I hated the place and got lost anytime I stepped outside any building. My bearings were saturated by signage I couldn't understand, by a language that felt impenetrable to all but those who were born with an innate knowledge of it in their DNA. Tokyo was the strangest and most alienating place I had ever visited. Even though I resided in the centre of London I felt constricted and claustrophobic under the weight of this megalopolis. There were always so many people everywhere and I didn't know any of them, nor did I feel I owned the capacity to communicate with them. They went about their business so quietly. No talking on the trains. Even though I was familiar now with sushi, the food there was so daunting and overwhelmingly exotic that I ate mostly at internationally-recognised fast food outlets. I went all the way to Japan to eat burgers and pizzas. Relief finally came by way of the gallery walls. I took my studies with me to Tokyo and hung them on the blank, pristine, white walls. It gave me a sense of reassurance to the task at hand. I began to plot and plan my montage of imagery. I started in pencil and when I had outlined all the compositions, I edited them with Japanese ink. There were characters from Manga, Anime and Video Games, Samurais, Geishas, Sumo Wrestlers, Salary Men, Yakuza, Buddhist Monks, Rockabilly Boys and Gothic Lolitas, Japanese Tourists, Japanese Drummers, Ninjas,

128

Kurasawa and Murakami, Yayoi Kusama, Nobuyoshi Araki, Tadao Ando, Sonny Chiba, Toshiro Mifune, Tojo, Noh Theatre, televisions, stereos, cameras, computers, cars, video consuls, a Bullet Train, a Zero Fighter with a Kamikaze Pilot, a mushroom cloud and a Hiroshima victim, neon signs in a Japanese script, cherry blossom, a tea ceremony, a paddy field, a bonsai tree, the Nakagin Capsule Tower and a Shinto shrine, Mount Fuji, sushi, beer, and saki. On the furthest wall was a Portrait of the Emperor benevolently seated with the Rising Sun behind him; the only part in colour. The whole thing was a hallucinogenic dream: a Pop art blur that continuously blended in and out of focus across the three walls.

The work was exhausting and felt like an endless task. When it was finally completed it stunned even me and I was its progenitor. The gallery owner was ecstatic. He hadn't visited the space during the entire time of creation. He had wanted to view it in its full splendour when the job was done. It should have been one of the most nerve-wracking moments of my entire career, but I was too tired and emotional to care. I got pissed on Japanese whisky, which I thought to be excellent. I took a case back home with me and meant to send a bottle up to my dad. I didn't find out he had died until I was back in London.

He had a heart attack at work. I'm told death was instantaneous. By the time the ambulance arrived, there was nothing left to be done. My mother held off informing me because she didn't want to ruin the exhibition. She also didn't know how to get hold of me. They called the apartment and I wasn't there. They didn't know the name of the gallery. It was all so typical; a series of miscommunications. I never went to the funeral. I cried off by claiming I had picked up some nasty bug out in Japan. There was nothing I could do. I had always tried to send my parents money, but they wouldn't take it. My mother wouldn't move to London and I wouldn't move back to Scotland. I would support her financially for the rest of her time here on earth. I would call once a week and attempt a dialogue of meaningful discussion which centred around the banalities of life, mostly the weather. The truth is, we had little enough to say to each other.

I always carried with me this intense feeling of guilt towards my parents. I was almost ashamed that I had achieved so much and they so little. I wished they had been happy, but I always remained unconvinced of that. For them, it may simply have been impossible. I loved my father, but I never missed him. There was never a time, as an adult, when I sought out his counsel. I don't know what he thought of me. My mother claimed pride. Perhaps that's true, but it may just as equally be false. As for her, I could never have saved her; life had already done its damage. Would a girl have helped? Instead of two selfish boys?

'He always said how proud he was of you, son. He didn't really understand art. We just weren't brought up like that. He didn't know what to say to you about it all. He didn't know how to help and encourage you.'

He alone remains, all too briefly. Holding empty space with hollow memories. You can see them all now with their eyes closed for eternity. Not a whisper emanates from deep in the dark void. He will join them all soon enough. None will last: none will endure. Human existence, in the end, shall prevail over all.

You made your way through the case of booze, prevaricating over a return to the studio. Each sip reminded you of Japan and your estrangement from it. London felt so monotonous. You longed for the surrealism of those neon and sweat-saturated streets. You missed that foreign smell and were eating sushi ravenously. You were haunted by a memory of her. She was sent to you by the gallery owner, who claimed you had a mutual friend. She appeared at the apartment with an introduction. She was pretty, in her late twenties, and had a pink bob. She said she was an erotic entertainer. You didn't understand what she meant. Was she a porn star or a prostitute? She carried with her a metal vanity case, with which she retired to the bathroom. When she reappeared she was wearing some sort of silver lingerie, shiny metal boots, and a fluorescent blue, strap-on dildo. She held in her hands some pink, silk, bondage rope. She took you to the bedroom and disrobed you. You offered no resistance. She told you to position yourself on the bed, on all fours. She bound your wrists and your ankles to the four corners of the bed. You allowed her to smear your anus with lubricant, before she mounted and began to ride you. She whispered Japanese words of encouragement, or consolation, sweetly in your ear. When you ejaculated, you came harder than you ever had in your life. You were shocked, scandalised, and unbelievably satisfied. So much so that you included her in the gallery drawing. You never spoke to the owner about it. You never spoke to anyone about it. He amusingly alluded to it before you left Tokyo. He said that Japan always surprised the visitor in ways they hadn't thought possible.

She stands there, a metallic android. She speaks indecipherable Japanese words, but she has no mouth. On a steel table a sushi chef peels back a crocodile's skin with a long, thin santoku knife, curling the scaly flesh around the blade. Underneath the skin, the flesh is the red ripe fruit of a watermelon. It is raining hard as the gallery owner kisses a Japanese woman sporting a full beard. An old, black-and-white Japanese gangster film is playing, on a gallery wall, replete with nonsense dialogue. Your father and brother drink whisky together in silence. He walks along a hot, crowded street. His brother, who is Japanese, is at an ATM playing a video game, which he pronounces to be 'rubbish'.

I had to return to the studio to produce more drawings and prints for the Japan show. There was a book completed and an accompanying television documentary, both titled: *Who is Nihon?* It was exhausting but exhilarating and I managed to avoid all the noise generated by the exhibition piece in Tokyo. There were the usual controversies, juxtaposing a war criminal with the emperor, the quality of the icons chosen, the ridiculous antiquated manner of the symbols of Japan.

'How can he put these images together?'

'This is just some half-assed *gaijin's* decrepit idea of Nihon.'

'It's all such a predictably stereotypical Western view of Japanese culture.'

I responded by stating they were a Western outsider's observation of Japanese culture and not an expression of how Japan viewed itself. The gallery owner was happy; it was a blockbuster show from his perspective. He even sold the piece itself, all three walls of it. I have no idea how they managed to remove it but it was reinstalled in a stockbroker's office. My cut was substantial and I suddenly realised I needed a studio assistant and a PA. I basically hired the first two people who came through the door, one with a fine art degree, the other with a business degree. I felt constricted; they were always waiting for new instructions. I wondered why I had hired them, but I also couldn't fire them, either. Eventually, after a few weeks, they settled in and pretty much defined their own roles for themselves. For my part, I took them to the pub every Friday lunchtime and got them drunk. I imagined that was what a good employer did. In all honesty, I found the whole staff thing incredibly intrusive. I said goodbye on a Friday and produced my work over the weekend and on Monday morning I became an administrator and facilitator again. But I finally got wise to the business end of things. I was owed monies from all over and I began to call in the cheques. It engendered a few trips to my solicitor's. I hadn't realised what a tough business the art world truly was. I railed at my studio assistants about crooks, scoundrels, thieves and brigands. I grew more bitter than ever. I was the talent and everybody made well off me, everyone except me. In reality, I was becoming rich, my stock was on the rise. I owned my flat, the studio rent and wages were always there, and I was earning far more income than I could spend. Yet those old demons remained. The slog had been too hard. Was any of it worth it? What was art, anyway, and who needed it?

'I'm the star, but the reality is I'm just a mere puppet, their financial patsy. All they have to do is to concentrate on bleeding me and prostituting me and pimping me out. Christ, I'm tired.' Typical of my drunken tirades in the pub.

The hollowness surrounding you had no demarcated edges, everything slipped helplessly into the chasm you had created. You phased out and stopped turning up. Your demeanour, in the studio, was lugubrious and dour. The drinking increased incrementally, you started to score heroin, and then your father's death slammed right into you. You gave your colleagues a week's holiday. You holed up in the studio with a case of Château Margot purchased from a vintners' in Chelsea and a wrap of smack procured from your drug dealer *du jour*. You drank, smashed bottles, cried, passed out, and burned holes in paper and canvas using lit ten-pound notes. You shook and rattled, vomited, pissed yourself - twice. On the Saturday evening you acquired a stolen bottle of Valium, took it home to the apartment in the Barbican, swallowed several pills, and half-heartedly attempted to commit suicide. You eventually puked until the lining of your stomach bled and you had to consider phoning for an ambulance, with the attendant threat of committal to a mental health facility. You pictured electric shock therapy treatment and balked. You stayed in bed for four days and ate two tins of soup. Your PA turned up and brought some shopping, lots of healthy goods. She chatted to you in the living room with you in your pyjamas. She listened to you, sympathised with you, left the flat, and then left her job.

I vacated the city for the seaside and a therapeutic change of air. I vacationed at the Headland Hotel in Newquay. A grand Victorian edifice with a commanding view of the sea, up on the promontory above the surfers' paradise of Fistral Beach.

I slept, watched television, drank afternoon coffee, took constitutional walks, ate supper. I made long sojourns along the sands of the town's many beaches. I visited the zoo and stared at the faces of the lonely animals. I visited its aquarium and witnessed the monotonous routines of its lonely sea life. I observed teenagers in wetsuits launch and hurl themselves off the harbour wall and into the cold green water below. At my hotel window I sat back for hours and watched the surfers grind and howl their way through rolling surf and sloppy beach-break. I craved an abandonment of everything: to be free of my role in life. To take solace in a quiet existence in reaction to the burdens of my career.

I first glanced at her walking along the beach wrapped in an expensive grey poncho. Her long, dark hair and those sparkling green eyes. She was a striking image on a chilled, grey and washed-out day.

I would later make claim to you that you were a heavenly vision at the centre of a sad and murky dream. We were both guests in a not yet quite in season hotel. We chatted over coffee a couple of times and then dined together one evening. You had just extricated yourself from a messy marriage filled with lies and deceit. A marriage you had never really countenanced. It was deemed beneficial to both families. I could never have understood such aristocratic ways. He seemed to have done financially well out of the whole arrangement. There we were in a washed-up early spring. We two lost souls clinging to one another. Never an auspicious beginning to any relationship.

I discovered rather quickly that she was nursing a cocaine addiction. She had been in and out of rehab facilities a few times with varying success, but was now doing cold turkey on her own terms. She was clean two months and six days when we first met.

Was she another of the lost causes you so earnestly pursued? The broken marriage, the dysfunctional family, the addiction; all fodder for your own innate alienation. Did you profit from it at all? Is art, in the end, simply a purveyor of human misery? You saw the struggle and the pain within her, but also the resigned arrogance and sense of entitlement inherent within her class. She was beautiful and damned: who could refuse her?

The dark is shimmering out over the eastern horizon. The blinding heat is on its ascent. The earth shall crack and quiver, break open in a monstrous evacuation of hard-baked soil. The burning winds, harsh and stinging, flaying the skins of human and livestock alike.

We started to meet up again back in London. She was temporarily living with a friend in a small flat in Kensington. She was estranged from her father at the time, due to the divorce. Her mother was married to a kiwi grower out in New Zealand and she hadn't seen her since her wedding. The mother had advised against the union as it had been a disastrous route for herself with the father. Her objections were discounted, much to the daughter's future chagrin. The relationship between them, never great to begin with, was further strained. She resented both her mother's protest at the union and prescience as to the future consequences of such a misalliance. As such, neither parent would recompense her, financially or emotionally, for the loss of wealth and status she suffered due to the termination of the marriage. She was on her own for the first time in her life, with only her own natural resources of bluff, guile, charm and beauty to see her through. She was living rent-free and was then currently employed in the guise of a receptionist at a traditional, commercial West End gallery, after which she swiftly relocated into the antique trade, of which she seemed to possess very little actual acumen. I admired her ingenuity and resilience; that cut-glass accent opened many doors in London and she prised ajar as many as she could.

I learned not to have unreasonable expectations of society. I had discovered, during the course of my life, that many people were loud, opinionated, obnoxious, ignorant, arrogant, and seemed mostly interested in an intense, supremely narcissistic form of self-preservation. The strong preyed on the weak and the weak in turn fed off the strong, in a never-ending battle over resources. I was a surrogate for this entropic system. I had galleries, dealers, collectors, curators, academics, critics, all bottom-feeding off my creative talents, and then I had her. Did she see me as an easy mark? The others were attracted to the artistic enterprise; they somehow believed in it. She placed her faith in survival. She was vain, conceited, pretentious, self-superior, but she also possessed a great worldly intelligence and determination and, crucially, she was extraordinarily loyal to me.

For somebody who was lodging with a friend, her taste ran from the expensive to the extravagant. She liked to shop in Harrods, Harvey Nichols, Liberty's, Fortnum and Mason, Bond Street, Knightsbridge and Chelsea boutiques. She indulged lunching at the swankiest of Mayfair eateries. If the will took her, she could have sunk a Greek shipping magnate in a matter of weeks. I discovered the well-bred, landed gentry were most excellent at spending other people's money, but not so great at generating it for themselves. They appeared to exist in an ulterior universe from the rest of society. Many seemed incompetent and inept, but socially, incredibly fluid. They entered every space as though they owned it, as if their ancestors conquered it hundreds of years before, through sheer force of superior will. Few of them seemed to do little of anything, except forge new schemes to have an income bestowed upon them. Their tastes were impeccable, they approached everything with a sort of nonchalant ennui, and everybody deferred to their top echelon, a priori, knowledge. The only matter of real interest to them was the social rank and standing of their peers. They gossiped endlessly about their own navel-gazing revue, of other aristocrats, in the same manner as us mere commoners would discuss footballers or celebrities. They were a large, utterly pointless, dysfunctional family. Whenever I heard politicians harping on about those in society who were unproductive, I always thought of the upper classes and not the underclass.

'Oh, Anthony always skis at this time of year in Chamonix with his mother.'

'Yes, and she always does the paying.'

'Of course she does, darling, he doesn't have a pot to piss in. Edward got the inheritance.'

'What there was of it. I heard there was only a few thousand left after death duties and he spent all that at the Gold Cup.'

'Her family kept all wealth. But then she always was the brains in that union.'

'Wouldn't have been difficult. God, they're a dreadful family. Such bores.'

I started to sketch her obsessively, almost immediately. She became a muse in ways all the others had never been. With them there was a strong intellectual determinant; they were intense and cerebral, or they were earthy, visceral and sexual. She was somewhat ethereal, as though she floated gaily through life, untouched and untroubled. Which wasn't true of her at all, but she always gave across that impression. She could be cantankerous, contrary and saturnine. She could also freeze the heart out of the sun with one glance. She was unhindered by the same social conventions as others. She had been sent to a convent school at a tender age and had acquired certain skills of self-reliance and self-critique. Her underlying judgements were formed almost exclusively, by herself, to her own credentials and specifications, and as such she was somehow separate from the world which she inhabited. She stifled approval, but when she condescended to offer some, it was fulsome in its praise. She was fun, flirtatious, and filled with bonhomie. She was also devious, covetous and wilfully obstinate. In the antiques trade she dealt in knowingly non-kosher items of dubious provenance. She had few scruples about fleecing some neophyte collector. It was mere transactions, barter and trade. She wanted cash and lots of it.

You were infatuated with her: the beauty, the mystery, the sensuality, the enigma; a true English rose. She dallied with you, pushed then pulled, crushed your hopes and then soared your spirits. Was she just another that liked to pull the wings off the boys? She boosted your career by driving a hard bargain. She could take on the most elite of them, without brains or brawn but with a toxic mix of mercurial charm and a steel-hard determination. You were in awe of her effortlessness, the way she guided and coaxed the world to her. She had been an event jumper, a fashion model, a business school graduate, a features editor at a national homes magazine. She had given it all up to marry and breed. She was infertile, that's what the doctor had declared. She lost an intimate part of her core self and discovered freedom in its place. She could have taken you for everything, but she didn't, and you never understood why.

Drawing upon drawing piled up in the studio over a period of a six-month courtship. She slept at my apartment often.

You were fearless before the sketchpad, you posed naked at will, eloquently draped over an armchair, in a bestial mass post-coital, motherly at a stove top, coquettish in the bath. You serenaded me sweetly into the bedroom and fucked with abandon. You listened intently and interjected with insight. You were mysterious with intimates and conspicuous with your affections for me. The word love held no bounds for you and was always readily within your reach. I always pictured you as a paradox. It's what I titled the exhibition: *I Dream You as a Paradox*. The final pieces on display were raw and visual, fragile epiphanies of beauty and flesh. They were hard-edged drawings in charcoal, ink and paint, with blacks, reds, pinks and the piercing emerald of your hypnotic eyes. Your long, lustrous hair; your vicious pout; your slender, curvaceous frame; your delicately poised composure; your dark, brooding form. The art was equal parts sensual and sexual. When you viewed the rough amalgam on the studio walls, pre-exhibition, you withheld your approval for several days. After the opening and initial flurry of art world and press interest in the new show, we decamped to the Amalfi coast. You sprung this Italian sojourn on me, fully booked and paid for, as a gift from you to me.

He lies perfectly still and pictures a giant vulture hovering overhead, silhouetted by the blue of the sky, like some ancient pterodactyl ready to feast on his flesh, the moment his eyes close for the final time. He envisages himself, mummified in shrouds, being lowered into the tomb, a small opening in the parched earth of the desert scrub. The mourners are all strangers from a far-off distant land. The place he now inhabits, so far from home and his ancestors. All that time and all those generations of Celts buried beneath the peaty soil, in small, scattered graveyards amongst mountains and lochs, rivers and glens.

How tragic and barbaric history all is, and how noble. Standing before the ruins of Pompeii with its timeless streets, its frescoes and its calcified corpses. A civilisation annihilated in one volcanic breath of nature. Mount Vesuvius, indomitable and eternal in the distance. The impossible afternoon heat stretched each footstep for an eon and there was a constant preoccupation with shade. Pompeii was perpetual; an iconoclastic wasteland in the Bay of Naples, but it may just as well have been Monte Cassino almost two millennia later, pounded by bombs and bullets into rubble. Human beings and nature, the earth's two great destructive and creative forces. I found myself astonished by it all, wondering how far we had really travelled. Was our civilisation so very different from theirs?

I brooded and mooched around Sorrento for the first few days. Schlepped up and down the hill to the hotel, in the draining heat, twice daily. I was bored and uncomfortable, the air-conditioning rattled on all night and the elevator clanked up and down. Italy never disappoints for long. The heat does wonders for the libido, mine and yours. We ate nightly at the restaurant of the little Enoteca; lots of gorgeous, tomato-based pasta, drank Falanghina and Limoncello. We walked through narrow, colourful streets, festooned with green, white and red bunting. Watched the old men play games in their social club. Ate a plate of penne with zucchini; that was one of the simplest and most wonderful meals I ever ate in my life. How clever they were with food. A lunchtime meal of *insalata alla caprese*, washed down with a cold Nastro Azzurro, in endless sunshine. What comfort, what joy. In the end, I felt I could have lived there forever. I stood and observed a man repairing a boat and imagined the timelessness of the place, of the Mediterranean, circling on forever. The birthplace of Western civilisation and the place where it may finally die. Globalisation had taken grip and the endless merging and reforming of cultures, no longer distinct from one another, but then a fatal synergised transaction of diminishing returns.

Why is peace so impossible to rescue from the world? A limitless expanse of subliminal silence. As though those ash-ridden shores would march on over the edge of the world into a cosmic nothingness. To wander the margins of time and to observe it warp, bend, and fold back in upon itself. A fourth dimension where the soul evaporates back into the womb of all creation. Perhaps in the outer reaches of the known universe there is an unimaginable quietness among the darkness which abounds.

You lay there supine on the bed, stretching and curling your naked form, as I drew you. An ancient nymph risen out of a timeless sea; an Anglo Saxon on the shores of the Med. You told me you loved me, then and there, for the first time. I responded in kind and then thought of those others. Why should this one be any different? Your eyes shone gallantly as the late afternoon light drifted in through the window with its diaphanous voile curtain. I saved that sketch for myself. It would always remind me of that moment. It was of little use to anyone else. Later, in the evening, when you were dressed for dinner, you pursed your made-up lips and left a deep red mark on the piece of paper on which you were drawn. We ate and drank and laughed, came home and made love, slept, and then awoke to a new dawn; our day of departure.

There you are. I've be searching for you. Squatting naked on the dusty floor of a Pompeii villa, she smashes a fresco with a stone. You ignore me as I pass. Outside, a waiter is filling the pool with wine. 'The sun stops in Winter,' he says. '*Presente Pompeii*,' I say. '*No si este Roma*,' he replies. 'Rome,' I glance around, 'of course.' 'It's Alessandro,' you say. 'I don't know him,' I answer. 'Yes you do,' she laughs. Alessandro passes her a bottle of Limoncello and she smashes it against Botticelli's *Venus*. The humidity is crushing as a yellow stickiness runs down the walls. I see the deep blue of the sky, an olive green, and a man swirling tomato spaghetti around in a bowl. 'It makes it taste better,' he says.

It rained at Gatwick, of course it did. I can still recall that damp, cool summer taxi ride back into town. The driver espousing all his right-wing views on the destitution of the empire. I almost demanded he drop us off half-way to our destination. You ignored him and put on some headphones. It did nothing at all to discourage his reactionary diatribe. You slept at my home and didn't leave.

You were content, or imagined you were, trooping off each day to the studio, returning to be with her. She could cook and suddenly your small kitchen was alive in the evenings: *coq au vin*, *boeuf bourguignon*, cottage pie, *moules marinière*, paella, macaroni and cheese, steak and chips, chicken parmesan, Lancashire hotpot and Cullen Skink, which she learned to cook just for you, even though you had never tasted it before. You began to run home from the studio in the evenings, to burn off the calories before you even had them. She liked to eat out plenty, too, at cheap and cheerful, at Michelin-starred, and everything in between. She always insisted on sharing the bill. You told her she should open a restaurant herself. She asked if you would back it, financially. You never answered and you never found out if she was serious or not. You escorted her to the opera, which she adored, but it was a spectacle you never fully got a liking for. She always played operatic music when she cooked and you held a great affection for those moments, if not the actual music. You admired the way she took simple pleasures and joys from little things: hot, soapy baths, buying a new pair of shoes, Wimbledon, antiques fairs, silk scarves, crime novels, tai chi, camomile tea, cut flowers and dachshunds, which you refused to own.

'They're stupid fucking things,' I say.

'You say everything's stupid,' she returns.

'But you can't even walk them properly. They get knackered after two steps. You can't run with them. You can't even wrestle them.'

'You can wrestle me if you like,' she states, teasingly.

'They're useless.'

'They're affectionate.'

The apartment started to fill at the weekends with friends over for supper: she was very politic as to who she invited. Chums who might be beneficial to my career, who could put in a word here and there, to help with sales. It was a dark, fractured world, which I never truly understood. A closed society of nuances and gestures between wealthy patrons from another class to mine. I had learned to mix well at gallery shows but this was something new. You could never quite tell where the power and influence lay. They were polite, of course, their manners were impeccable. I drank and said little in their presence and always got shit-faced when they had left. She never quarrelled, but left me to it. In her own way she must have understood. It festers, though, over time; it spoils and turns rotten. I would leave the flat on my peregrinations, late in the night, drink alone in bars, take taxi rides around London. One November morning I awoke to the dank, stale smell of the putrid autumnal leaves in Regent's Park. I was shivering with the cold beneath a large, forbidding tree. In my jacket pocket was a gram of cocaine, which I had no memory of acquiring.

I arrived home at eight in the morning and you were spare with worry. You mentioned rehab, counselling, AA, but I breezily rebuffed you and refused them all. I asked if you wanted to leave and you cried, called me a bastard, then left the apartment and didn't return until late that evening. I snorted the coke while you were gone, watched *Scarface* for amusement, then showered and went to bed. I got back up again a week later and we stopped having supper parties.

'What's wrong?' you ask.

'What do you mean?' I answer.

'You always carry this monkey on your back. As though you're somehow trying to escape something; yourself, perhaps. It doesn't matter how fast you move, or how well you hide, it always keeps pace and always discovers your secret place.'

'I'm just me.'

'Don't you trust me? Why won't you let me help?'

'Who can help?'

'Me. I can,' you say tenderly.

In the dark still of the approaching dawn, which crackles off out in the distance, across a continent, the cattle are becoming restless. The density in the air begins to respond subtly, to a rumbling furnace, which will soon enough engulf all. The herdsmen slumber on; there is time yet, before the day will open fully and beckon them forth to their labours.

You looked so peaceful when you slept, so elegant and gorgeous, I never knew how you did it. I kept a sketchpad by the bed always. I used it on you often in the pale, early morning light, entering the room for the first time each day. You used and then stopped. I admired your self-control; a couple of drinks and that was all. You didn't seem to need it and then increasingly less so, as time went on, as old wounds healed, as therapy progressed. I think you grew stronger as I grew weaker. You were always willing to carry me with you. Why did you love me? Why wasn't that enough?

Your estrangement from your father seemed to end. You had gradually reinstated contact with him and for those purposes we paid him a visit at his estate in Oxfordshire. Where his sole income, pleasure, hobby and obsession was breeding racehorses. His only other interest appeared to be in killing things: ensnaring, fishing and shooting them. For me, he was one giant caricature, as I was in turn for him. I drew him as a toffee-nosed country oaf and he referred to me as Karl Marx, or The Draughtsman. We both got along just swell.

He asked me if I did any grouse-shooting up in the Highlands, or deer-poaching. I thought he was a fucking lunatic for asking, but said I did some fishing. That seemed to set him off, lecturing me about fly-fishing for salmon. I couldn't have cared less about his hunting expeditions or his stupid horses. I advised you I was terrified of the animals because I was almost kicked in the head by one as a child.

'Horses are more intelligent than most people, you know,' he confides.

'Really.' I make no effort to conceal my disbelief in his ludicrous theories.

'Oh yes, very intelligent animals. Very superstitious, too. It sets us apart, you know.'

'What does?'

'Horses.'

'How's that, then?'

'Well, no other animal that I know of uses another animal they way we use horses; for company, for friendship, for transport, for labour, for recreation.'

'No. Then I don't suppose many other animals can paint, either.'

'My God, your father's fucking tonto,' I tell you later.

'Why, what was he saying?' you ask suspiciously.

'He was saying loads of crazy shit about horses.'

You laugh, 'He's obsessed with the bloody things.'

You took me out to the stables to let me pet your favourite on the nose; it never cured me of my phobia. You were different out in the countryside, you hardened noticeably in his presence. He respected your stoicism, your sense of survival, your noble breeding and your unwavering defence of your parvenu companion.

You stalked around in wax jackets and jodhpurs, went out riding twice-daily for the few days we visited. I watched you from afar, from up at the leaded bedroom window. You galloped across the fields, supremely confident at the reins. He advised me as to the pictures of ancestors hanging on the walls, which were all painted by some society hacks. At the head of the table, in the grand dining room, was a portrait of the queen on which, on the second night, while drunk, I was sorely tempted to draw a comedy goatee. You would have killed me, then laughed all the way back to London. I wandered through the house freely when you and your father were at the stables. I searched his crystal brandy decanter for pen marks at the fluid height. I sensed he wasn't worth that much money. In the evenings, chatting, he had a kind of slightly morose quality to him, as though he realised his best days were past. He confided to me that he was sleeping with the mother of your ex-husband. That he hadn't had the courage, nor the conviction, to break it off after your divorce.

You confided to me that you had lost your virginity to one of the stable hands. On a bed of hay, like something out of a cheesy romance novel. He spread his conquest around the local village and humiliated you. When you confronted him about his lack of gallantry and got into a contretemps, he insulted you vulgarly so you struck out, in anger, with a riding crop. He retaliated by punching you to the ground, then promptly left your father's employ. You had a large facial bruise which you thought was caused by a broken cheekbone. You told your father you had been thrown by your horse. He marched you out to the stables and made you jump up on the saddle immediately, to control and dominate the beast, ride it hard across the fields and show it no fear. Your mother suspected differently; as did your older brother, who sought out the fellow in question and hospitalised him. It was all of little consequence to you. You had been wronged and it couldn't be righted. You underestimated him. You thought he would have treated you better. You said it was a pattern that would develop. I wasn't sure if that meant me. In that moment, I would have given anything for it not to have been.

We left Oxfordshire with your father declaring to you that I seemed an amiable enough chap and wishing you well in your future happiness. You were a little sad and disconsolate for the first few days when we returned home. You missed the country; I hated the place.

Your father stomps around a muddy field firing his shotgun in the air. 'All these bloody pigeons,' he says, 'I'm hunting for spatchcocks.' You're in a hay barn, but you can't find your car keys. You have a whip in your hand made from a dead branch. 'I can hit you if you want,' you say, 'Daddy won't mind. He can't hear.' The Queen's portrait is above the fireplace in our apartment. 'It's the one the Sex Pistols used,' you say, 'it's worth a fortune now.' You're playing Puccini and plucking a pheasant. 'Like we had back home,' I say. 'Did you?' you ask. 'My father liked them,' I reply. 'I didn't know your brother,' you state. I take a syringe full of heroin and squirt it across the coffee table as you begin to sing.

I kicked around vacantly for some time, unsure as to my next project. I sketched pointlessly in the studio and sipped orange juice and espresso at a local Italian café, which I had begun to frequent. I would sit and watch films at home in the afternoons, then nap until you returned home. We would take long walks together through the departed city at the weekends, destitute of its brokers and bankers. I became sedentary overnight. It wasn't energising, but it was relaxing. I felt life slowing down, beginning to pace itself more. I kept in touch with my gallery, fed them some bullshit about grand plans. We went shopping together and I started to cut a dash through the art world, with snappy suits, shirts and scarfs. You acquired a look for me, which I became noticeable for. We joined a gym and worked out twice a week, on Wednesday evenings and Sunday afternoons. I even took tennis lessons and played the occasional doubles match with you and some of your friends. You liked to play the odd game of Scrabble on cold, dark winter nights and you taught me how to play backgammon. Life was nice; uncomplicated, sober and sedate. I thought I might get a genuine feel for it. Living like other people; normal folks. I had never really imagined that type of life for myself, and had always approached it with a mordant fury. To be an artist, after all, was to be fucked up. Why should I have lived like others? An artist lives for their art and their art alone. It is the only relationship which matters.

Do we seek to destroy ourselves; anatomise our being? The power of destruction, to annihilate and obliterate our corporeal selves. To metamorphose into a vanquished state of single-cell nuclei. Mere vapours floating among the vague currents in the ether. We have then returned to our essential state of non-being.

You insisted you were happy, content with your place in the world. It takes some people a long time to discover their true selves. You told yourself that this was you, that it had always meant to be. Your destiny had arrived in a different guise as to that which you had expected. It was all there for the taking, you only had to reach out and grab it all for yourself. The malaise ripples endlessly under the skin. It seeks you out at every turn. Art isn't created through an ease of touch; it is a bastard, in a bloated and bloodied, permanently pregnant, form.

You hustled me a commission. An old school friend had managed to wed herself to a wealthy Russian businessman whose sister wanted to open a new, contemporary art gallery in Moscow. He was making container-ship-sized deposits of cash from natural gas resources and had kicked some over to his sibling for her amusement. She had an art history degree and actually turned out to be a very intelligent and astute connoisseur of art. My other galleries were extremely nervous about dealing with such a fledgling enterprise. Comments were made to me about the provenance of the money involved, which amused you greatly; the hypocrisy was staggering in the extreme. Some of the interjections were quite frankly offensive and xenophobic, and pushed me firmly into her new gallery's welcome arms. In truth I had my own reservations; the thought of Russia terrified me. I had grown up during the Cold War and some of the propaganda of those times, mixed in with the more contemporary horror stories of the Russian mafia, were enough to drive on a growing sense of reluctance and then outright paranoia about the place. Unlike previous shows, I decided to complete the work in Blighty first, then ship the framed pieces to the gallery in Moscow to be hung in situ. I never explained the reason for operating in such a manner, rather than my usual method of creating drawings direct onto the gallery walls, but she was perfectly fine with that arrangement. You were the go-between and smoothed everything over with her.

I worked for six months tirelessly on that inaugural exhibition titled: *Mother Russia and the Bear*. You purchased for me copies of *The Brothers Karamazov*, *Anna Karenina*, and *The Seagull*. I kept falling asleep reading Dostoyevsky; I watched a film version of Tolstoy, but managed to make my way through the Chekhov, and enjoyed it enough to visit the theatre to see a stage production of it. The premise of the show was simple enough; each image fitted into the next, using the metaphor of the Russian Doll. There was a full Pantheon of a Westerner's guide to the country: Alexander Nevsky, Ivan the Terrible, Peter the Great, Catherine the Great, Nicholas II, Lenin, Trotsky, Stalin, Khrushchev, Brezhnev, Gorbachev, Russian icons, Russian serfs, Cossacks, Russian soldiers, Russian athletes, ballerinas,

Kandinsky, Chagall, Soutine, Malevich, Tatlin, Dovzhenko, Rodchenko, Pudovkin, Eisenstein, Dziga Vertov, Tarkovsky, Stanislavski, Nijinsky, Nureyev, Diaghilev, Stravinsky, Shostakovich, Tchiakovsky, Gogol, Pushkin, Dostoyevsky, Tolstoy, Chekov, Turgenev, Solzhenitsyn, Boris Spassky, Anatoly Karpov, Garry Kasparov, Yuri Gagarin, Marshall Zhukov, the Hammer and Sickle, nuclear warheads, Sputnik, the T34 Tank, a Lada and a Red Star were all fitted exponentially into a great, roaring, all-powerful Russian Bear, to produce one single image of an overall collective montage. Any subtlety or irony intended within the work was lost in those resurgent times. I had never travelled to Russia and I knew nothing of the Russians as people. They had been beaten down after the fall of the Berlin Wall but, as Russia is wont to do, it resurrected itself in quick time, to reassert its rightful position as a global power once more.

The moment I landed at Sheremetyevo Airport, my pulse rate seemed to increase tenfold. I was in the lair of the beast, the land of superspies and torture chambers, of purges and summary executions. I was convinced that, as a subversive Western artist, I would be tailed and hounded by my own designated detachment of the security services. My driver held my name on a board at the arrival gate as I was advised he would. It was mid-November and the moment we left the airport terminal, a blast of cold air, the likes of which I had never experienced in my life, even in the Scottish Highlands, hit me full in the face, like a solid-ice brick. I panicked for a second time. How could any one human withstand such cold? Fortunately, the high-end Mercedes in which I was driven to the Hotel Metropol had full heating. When I exited the vehicle in front of the hotel, that dense frozen air hit me fully for a second time; it was literally unbearable. Once ensconced in my room, I amused myself and calmed my nerves by searching the space for old-style Cold War bugs, à la James Bond. I found none and my entire trip went as smooth as it possibly could have. I was given the whistle-stop tourist tour of the city, from the Kremlin and Red Square to

Saint Basil's and the Bolshoi. I was shown Lenin's tomb, Shukhov's tower, and Gorky Park. I observed the people in the street, from the comfort and warmth of the car. Imagining them at the other side of that great cultural and political divide; the Iron Curtain. I discovered the historical constant, that the West had always underestimated the sophistication of the Russians, the cultural elite were not simply enriched peasants and workers, though like most formally impoverished people they were inclined towards bling. I found them to be extraordinarily gracious company; witty, intellectual, and gregarious to a fault. They were effusive in their hospitality. With them, your glass or plate was never empty. No request seemed too outrageous and they were willing to step on their ego to accommodate you. It wasn't always easy to discern what was going on and the person you thought was in control always seemed to defer to someone else. It was difficult to anchor just where the power resided. None of this affected my position or stature whatsoever; I was treated with deferential amiability. I was wined and dined all over Moscow, at fine dining establishments, trendy new bars, and a lapdancing club. I was given copious amounts of vodka, the best I had ever tasted; although I was reliably informed the Swedes made the best, I concurred equally unpatriotically that the Japanese made the best whisky. They refused to countenance that one. They had uppers and downers and a deft line in Russian models for hire. I didn't partake, for fear of being trapped in some elaborate state-run sting operation.

'You are confused by us, my friend. You have read all that nasty Western propaganda about us being savages. Well, perhaps some of it is true. Russia is a puzzle wrapped in an enigma, with gorgeous prostitutes and nuclear warheads,' one journalist roars with laughter.

The Moscow exhibition was a sell-out on its first night. There were three versions of every drawing produced and a number of limited edition prints. The Soviets were so starved of modern art for so long, being pedalled a constant array of girl-meets-tractor, socialist-realist tosh, that they were desperate to buy up any contemporary art going. I was told the Russians always made you money. I made a killing. The gallery cut was only a risible twenty-five percent. You negotiated that. I came home flush, the money had cleared before I even landed in London. It was unheard of in the art world. What a way to do business. The rest of the galleries were making a rube out of me. I held them in even greater contempt after dealing with the Russians.

You couldn't have been more delighted to see me. You threw your arms around my neck and kissed me with heart-melting tenderness. We went home and slept together, then stayed in bed for a whole weekend, venturing outside the confines of the bedroom only to forage for provisions. I wanted you more than ever. To lie naked, enclosed in your motherly embrace. To forget about all past indignities and all future indiscretions. I wanted to stay with you forever; I still do.

The dark knows nothing, except for an infinite blackness. When I know death, it will be a lie. I will atrophy all exertions. I will desist from all motion. I will render all memories invalid. I will simply cease to be.

That spring, we vacationed in Norfolk, in a little family chalet by the sea, which you rented from a friend. We drove there in your zippy silver Audi TT, which bumped precariously along the narrow beach road leading to the property. You said you had always dreamed of owning a Porsche, but your husband wouldn't let you buy one. I got you a surprise that summer, the red 1980s Cabriolet version you desired. I took you outside with your eyes closed and warned you: no peeking. I had put a big bow on it. You squealed with joy when you saw it and held a magical child-like look in your eyes when I passed you the key.

'Oh darling, it's wonderful,' you scream, 'I love you so much.' You kiss me passionately.

I was so glad to make you happy. I wanted you to have everything you ever wished for. We walked along the chill beach together. Our bare feet sinking into the cold sand. We reminisced of our first meeting in Cornwall.

I lay and read a biography of Mikhail Bakunin while you went out and foraged for bread and wine. We took a boat trip through the mighty broads and I fantasised about living there, having a little Riva speedboat tethered at the end of the garden, to go in to pick up the newspaper on a Saturday morning. I would have liked to have lived there by the water. You warned me that is was totally impractical because I couldn't swim. Then suggested we move down by the river in London as a surrogate.

She persuaded you to move but you weren't convinced; all that mattered was the space to create. She found you both a magnificent flat on Cheyne Walk and a new studio in Fulham. You passively went along with the whole plan, she arranged everything. You couldn't say no by then.

Her mother visited from New Zealand and gave her some money to help with her share of the cost of the purchase. She busied about renovating the place, all the fixtures and fittings; building a home for the two of you.

You sat and sulked in your new studio. You had become unaccustomed to change. You said it affected your creative output.

You had nothing to say.
    'This whole thing has disrupted the flow,' I say.
    'What flow?'
    'My work.'
    'I thought you said you couldn't create at the moment. Well, this will give you space to regroup.'
    The mother was suntanned and good-looking, like the daughter. She had a nice life out in the Antipodes with her husband and your brother, who ran the estate for them. She missed her daughter and hinted that we could move out to

New Zealand and have a better life. You demurred and said you were happy in England. Your husband had been a scoundrel, bankrupted you both, gambled in casinos and slept with strippers and any others that came along. You admitted he once passed on to you something nasty and unmentionable. Between the lawyers and the clinics, it all ended in ruin. You were still raw about it and fragile in your own way, both ferociously confident and tremendously insecure.

I found you puzzling at times; you were cold and remote, and warm and affectionate. I was loving and belligerent, passionate and despairing. How do any relationships last?

There was a young man in the street, who sat often by an alleyway with his bedraggled mongrel dog faithfully by his side. I chatted with him a few times. He grew up in children's homes and foster care, had been in and out of minimum-wage jobs and social housing, squats, and spent a stint in prison for drug offences. His girlfriend had died from a heroin overdose six months before and he went into freefall and got thrown out of their bedsit in White City. Like me, he had drifted down to the river. I bought him coffees occasionally and slipped him the odd fiver or tenner. One Arctic snap in January I let him kip in the studio for two days while the worst of the weather passed. He quietly slipped away one morning and I never saw him again. I looked for him and asked around but nobody knew anything, he simply disappeared back into the scrum and throng of the city.

'As long as I keep clean, I'll be doing fine,' he said, 'I'll meet her again soon enough.'

Keeping clean, keeping clean, sometimes that's all it comes down to.

His groans are almost imperceptible. The darkness grows blacker as the dawn approaches. A new day will arise which he will never witness. We do not choose our moment of passing, it chooses us. There are no words or incantations which can confine and confirm us to this world. We each of us must die and we must die alone. He knows little of what surrounds him anymore, he cannot feel or sense the world of which he remains an occupant.

Reality does not define us; we define reality. It bends to our will. Art does not mirror reality; reality is shaped by art. Nothing can enter the world which has not first been through the senses. I struggled on in the studio unable to produce. I worked in oils, black on black: in memoriam Malevich. I couldn't get his presence out of my mind; what courage, what genius. Between them all, they killed art before we even had a chance. What else was there left to produce; left to say? I ate fish and chips, or steak and onion pie, in the pub at lunchtimes, supping at a pint of micro-brewed real ale. I read *The Morning Star*, which I subscribed to at the local newsagents. I awaited the revolution; it never came. From each according to their means to each according to their needs. I proclaimed social revolution to be the panacea for all of society's ills. You said it was just a mild form of artistic ennui. I said I was tired of being ruled over by one scumbag after another.

'What is it you want?' she asked me. 'These people come to pay homage to your work and you spit at them. They've made you famous. They've made you rich and yet you despise them still. You don't live on a housing scheme with crime and poverty and rats. You live in Chelsea. They helped you get here. Why do you hate them so much? If you feel so bad, with some class-guilt thing - which I can understand, it's perfectly rational - then give away some money, to charity, or a political cause.'

'I do that already,' I stated morosely.

'Then stand for parliament. Do something else to effect change. You say you're burnt out and fed up with art anyway. Do something different for a change. I'll stand by you no matter what. I'm not a reactionary. I don't want people to go hungry or homeless any more than you do. I voted Labour at the last election,' she concluded.

The new prestigious address hastened the arrival of more supper clubs and I began to stay out later. I had no respect at all for those countrified debs and city gents you cultivated. Every one of my world had scattered to the winds, settled down to a cosy bourgeois existence, squirreling away in the studio, trying to pay the mortgage and win that big, international prize that was eluding them. The *nouvelles vagues* kept washing up on the shore, pushing the older generation far from the watering hole. I wondered why anyone would care anymore. They awarded me some things along the way, of course they did. They didn't wish to be seen as cultural ingrates. The judges knew nothing of art, but everything about posturing and posing. I detested them; I detested them all.

Los Angeles called again. My gallery wished to run a sort of mini retrospective of my career so far. I leapt at the chance to leave that mournful city I now inhabited. The blue of the sky, the red of the sun, the green of the ocean, blossomed once more into full consciousness, from the edge of a continent. I persuaded you not to go; my gallerist had died and his daughter was severely proprietorial about her artists. I told you she was an asshole, but I had to cultivate her patronage. You called me a sycophant and teased me mercilessly for two weeks prior to departure.

'Oh, it's the tortured artist. The man who is going to lead his class out of the desert. Boo, hiss, to all those mean little capitalists, who steal all your money and make you hole up in that nice studio all day with no bosses or deadlines and make you live in that big apartment with that horrible, beautiful woman that gives the best fellatio in the world.'

You still secured me a better percentage with her. When I arrived in LA, I drove down Santa Monica Boulevard towards the ocean and wondered why I had departed the time before. How wonderful it must have been to exist in permanent sunshine. It rained for the first three days I was there. It was unseasonable weather. It felt like October to me.

My gallery had insisted on collecting an edition of all my

completed work. They believed in me and threw themselves behind my career. They were to hold the exhibition in their Los Angeles gallery, but they had just purchased an industrial-sized space in London. They wanted me to show for their inaugural exhibition. They wanted to hold a mid-career retrospective of my work with a new, large mural installed on site. They fêted me across the city, rolled out the red carpet, invited some celebs to the show. I mulched about, sipping champagne and attempting to charm all in my path. I'm not sure my heart was really in it. I stayed two weeks in LA, did print, radio and television interviews, visited some parties and the Griffith Observatory. I told the gallery I would return to the city the next time and produce a large montage, as a curling stream of celluloid, featuring all the movers and shakers, divas and drivers of Hollywood's illustrious history, and all the little people they stood on to get there. They claimed to be overjoyed with the prospect. I suspect they were just humouring me at that stage in the mounting. They weren't when the show sold out. My work was now hanging on the walls of some prestigious addresses in the Hollywood hills and Malibu, Palos Verdes and Pacific Palisades.

I hooked up with a journalist for a music magazine, who was headed up to San Francisco to write a piece on a new band making waves in the hipster community up there. I tagged along for the fun and the adventurous spirit of the Beats. We drove up the coast road in her beaten-up, old, acid-yellow Beetle. I offered to pay for the rental of a reliable vehicle but she refused, claiming it would antagonise the soul of her car, which would then stop performing altogether. She had owned it for five years and it was held together with rust and love. It made it to Santa Barbara before collapsing dead on the highway. We stayed the night in a cheap motel and then hired a Ford in the morning. She arrived in the City a day late for the interview; the band had already moved on to perform a gig in Portland that night, so she interviewed a different group instead. This band were shacked up in the basement of a tech entrepreneur from Silicon Valley, in the affluent Pacific Heights district. From the house itself there was a great view of the ocean but they seemed to live like slobs in its discarded underbelly. We partied with them all the same, drank some Wild Turkey and dropped some MDMA. We went to a couple of music clubs, I think, then on to a party out in Berkeley, which had wound up before we reached there at dawn. We ate tacos and burritos for breakfast before we dumped the hire car and flew back to LA.

I had that usual grizzled London feeling in my stomach when I returned home; always the same when rerouted from sparklingly bright California. They do razzmatazz better than anyone. Europe always looks in a state of terminal decline and depression after visiting America; no wonder they run everything. I lived in a gilded world and the close-quarter grime of London always penetrated that. My life was all a vacuous and frivolous fantasy. One day I would awake from it all to discover a planet in ruin and desolation. Destruction was ever part of the double-headed Janus of creativity and that dichotomy always pulsed through me.

You picked me up from the airport and after a twelve-hour snooze we slept together, then in a state of wild contentment went out for a pleasant meal. We drank a little champagne cocktail and some Beaujolais, then chatted about LA and the show.

'Maybe we should move out there,' you said.

'To LA?' I asked, puzzled.

'Yes. You say it always sunny and warm, unlike London. There's nothing really to hold us here. You've got contacts and some cultural traction over there. Who knows, maybe I could be a film producer or something? Sell antiques to the stars. They like to feel classy, don't they? We could be happy together, out there in the sunshine.' She snuggled into me.

During a pleasant evening at home, several weeks later, in a bout of drunken incompetency and stupidity I confessed that I had fucked the journalist and that a soap opera actress had gone down on me in a hot tub at a party at a Bel Air mansion.

Why do such a thing? Why admit it? Somehow, I imagined that you would understand. That we were bohemians and not exclusively committed to one another. You slapped me hard across the face then told me to leave our home.

Did I wilfully self-sabotage? Was that forever to be my modus operandi? A detestation of being loved and being needed.

She changed the locks in the flat, sent your clothes over to the studio and had them dumped outside by a taxi driver. By the time you received her text about it, they had been stolen. You bought a single mattress, a duvet and some bedding, which you set up by the kitchen area in the studio. You sat and listened to Chet Baker, Charlie Parker, Miles Davis, Dizzy Gillespie, Thelonious Monk, Dave Brubeck and John Coltrane; the music of your father. How he would sit on his own at the little formica table in the kitchen, smoking cigarettes and listening to jazz programmes on the radio. You had a wall filled with photographs you had taken over the years, from around the world, mostly black and white: a montage of your travels. You lay on the floor for days and stared at them. They all looked the same, as though they had been taken in the same place. What difference was there between Rome and Tokyo, California and Cornwall? They were images from a past that was dead, from a mortality which could not be resurrected. You pondered what your father's face must have looked like when he gulped down his last: what his final expression was. You had trouble describing his face to yourself and you scrambled for a photo. It was an old one of him smiling, wearing a purple paper hat, extending half a Christmas cracker; the short end. You wanted to grip hold of his strong arms, burned by the weak Scottish sun. You wanted to burry your head in his chest and weep. You opened the top-grade Swedish vodka, sent to you by a writer friend in Russia, in exchange for a bottle of exclusive Japanese whisky. You drank it all, got sick, then ordered out for some more. You could get anything in

London, at any time of the day. You fell in love with the city all over again.

Who can survive in this unforgiving landscape? Who can endure such a fate? Millennia of pain and suffering and struggle and penance. For what sins? I was back closer to the cradle of existence, from whence we all came and migrated to other lands. It is here, in the land of our forefathers, I shall expire and remain as a part of the eternal dust of this pock-ridden earth.

I abandoned the studio and wandered around England's green and pleasant lands. I was in touch with an old pal from university, from the days of student halls. He had married a farmer's daughter up in Yorkshire and he invited me to stay with them for the weekend. His wife disappeared off with the two kids to his mother's in Fife, so we were free to indulge ourselves. The stench of excrement was excruciating, but there was an upside to things. As a sideline on the farm, my old friend grew the most fantastic skunk. Real potent, hallucinogenic stuff. We smoked spliff after joint and drove his big Massey Ferguson tractor around a fallow field. After which, we staggered back to the farmhouse and drank bottles of local ales and listened to rock music from the Seventies; Pink Floyd, Led Zeppelin, David Bowie, Frank Zappa, The Grateful Dead, all at full volume. I whited out and sat motionless in an armchair for two hours, before devouring some pork stew made with a pig from the farm, which had been recently slaughtered.

I talked to him about you. I told him your great, great grandfather started it all off with a greengrocers shop in Leeds. He said the shop was still there with your surname above it. Your mother's family were successful dairy farmers in Devon. They had the money. Your father's father had drunk most of the fortune - gathered over two generations - away by the time your papa came of age. He was expensively educated, but that was about all. Your grandfather died of sclerosis of the liver, your grandmother from the disappointment she had passed on to her son. My friend counselled that the country life was a hard one and that he himself had married into it by accident. He was bored and lonely, couldn't stand the other Tory-wielding boors and bores that surrounded him. He surreptitiously enquired whether I might be buying a new place in London with a spare bedroom. Then he desperately offered to take over as my studio manager. I advised him that I didn't have one, that I once had a crew but they had all abandoned ship. That art for me was a singular, failed pursuit. I offered to lend him some money, but that wasn't what he needed. What he needed was what he alleged I had: freedom.

'You don't know what it's like. It's an endless round of misery and graft, followed by more misery and further graft. If it's not the farm, it's the kids. Don't have children, for Christ's sake. They're so fucking boring. Got to take them to this party, this outing, pick them up from school. All they ever do is take. I can't remember the last time I had sex. The boy gets scared and insists on sleeping in our bed, with us. I've started sleeping in the spare room. I doubt the marriage will last much longer. She's probably up there consoling with my mother right now about her useless fucking son. We've got so much debt. I just want to sell the place and be done with it,' he slurs, stoned.

'Do you want me to invest in it? Help you out,' I offer lamely.

'No, no, no, don't be daft. It would just be throwing good money after bad. It's a fucking money pit. I just want out of it. I'm so fucking tired of it all.'

Remember that you too will die. Immortality is always at the back of the mind for the artist. There is the knowledge that all of this stuff is ephemeral, just like the flesh and blood. Nobody truly knows what part of any of it will survive. History has a surfeit of geniuses who never made the grade.

You wandered on carelessly from place to place, by train, bus and taxi, to Manchester, Bristol and Cardiff. You sought out old friends and former comrades, some who remembered you, others who had forgotten they knew you. One looked confused for a moment then realised he knew you from a television documentary and was surprised and delighted by how well you were making out. He was an art teacher in a secondary school. He kept a small, well-maintained studio with his wife, also an art teacher, but at a sixth form college. They were committed socialists with two children, both teenage boys. You took them all out for a slap-up meal at a fancy burger joint. They were charming company all evening and you delighted in watching their brimming family dynamic. You sketched them on a napkin and signed it, buoyantly joking to the lads that it would pay for their education. It was a gesture to hide the clumsiness of your intrusion into their iconoclastic world. The whole episode left you drunk on cheap wine in a dreary, corporate, chain hotel near the motorway. You couldn't distinguish between the rancid anguish of your life or the apparent mediocrity of their ambitions. You gave vent of your spleen to the walls until an exhausted-looking, porn-riddled salesman knocked on the door to quieten you down. You offered him a drink but he declined and wandered arbitrarily back to his ancient laptop and free Wi-Fi.

I arrived back in London with a restless feeling of faux homelessness. I consulted with the gallery and they intervened and located me a studio and loft apartment in an old Victorian building in Peckham. They organised a removals van as I holed up, terminally pissed, in a Park Lane hotel. I was back to a double mattress on the floor, two Marcel Breuer Wassily chairs, an iPod and dock, a MacBook, three pots and pans, three bowls, two plates, a knife and fork, four cups and saucers, an expensive Italian coffee machine, which I couldn't operate, and a cafetière. I immediately purchased the holy trinity of kitchen appliances: a fridge/freezer, a washing machine and a dishwasher. I was set for life. I calculated that with current and future earnings

I could live a comfortable and long existence.

Careerwise, I was being offered a guest slot on a new-format TV programme, judging amateur artists' drawing skills, which I immediately turned down. It was also whispering around the art world that I was being considered to represent Britain at the Venice Biennale. My stock would bloom after that and everyone that had ever shook hands with me, never mind purchased any of my work, was praying for that gig to come off. A gallery in Perth, Australia, wanted to commission me for a show. I semi-facetiously suggested hanging a dozen aboriginal artworks as found objects and calling the show: *I am Australia*. The gallery declined and the Australian press found out about it and had a grand debate on the issue, which I was never consulted on, nor asked to be a participant in.

The only offer I found remotely intriguing came several months later, for a show in Vienna. I buried my head in the studio, purchased a new assistant, and began the long process of producing prototype drawings to be copied onto the walls of the Viennese gallery.

I took up residency in a hotel suite a short walk from the gallery and with my new assistant proceeded to create my latest installation entitled: *Heroes and Villains*. I had built, to my own specifications, a labyrinthine maze in the gallery. On each large panel I completed the face of an Austrian personality, rendered in an exceptionally precise three-dimensional format. The space surrounding them was dark, but the portraits themselves were classically lit. There were a broad mix of suspects: Mozart, Bach, Strauss, Schubert, Mahler, Arnold Schwarzenegger, Otto Preminger, Billy Wilder, Fritz Lang, Josef von Sternberg, Erich von Stroheim, Egon Schiele, Josef Fritzl, Archduke Franz Ferdinand, Harry Lime, Ernst Kaltenbrunner, Marie Antoinette, Maximilian Schell, Romy Schneider, Oskar Werner, Gustav Klimt, Ferdinand Porsche, Ludwig Wittgenstein, Sigmund Freud, Rainer Maria Rilke and Simon Wiesenthal. The journey ended with a ruthlessly lifelike composition of Adolf Hitler.

The mainstream and right-wing Austrian press were livid over the exhibition and prosecuted an endless supply of arguments to have it totally shut down to the public. They called it a monstrous aberration of Austrian culture, which had enraptured the world. They also argued that Hitler was a citizen of Germany and a product of that country's politics, history and culture, not Austria's. The institution fought a losing battle and, after a week and a half, ordered the final offending panel to be removed. It was transported to a gallery in Dusseldorf and put on public display there to lesser controversy. Both shows were an enormous success, motivated by all the free advertising, proving the adage that there is no such thing as a bad press. My gallery was delighted and sketches, drawings, prints and copies of Hitler were sold out immediately. A book on the exhibition, as an estimable addendum to the catalogue, was hastily produced and immediately went out of print. Amid all this art world furore, I was informed that my mother had died. That she had alighted to bed early as usual and died in her sleep of a massive stroke, the very same kind that did for her father.

He groans noiselessly under a damp, soiled sheet. There are no further secretions: no blood, no urine, no excreta, no tears. He is a biological mass in a state of formal collapse. He is crawling, without motion, towards his grave. He is death rendered mortal. He will not survive this night.

You fell into a still blackness. A nightmare between the real and the unreal. A mother already rotting in the grave next to the eviscerated corpse of your father and the fish manure of your brother. You swallowed uppers and downers washed down with whisky and wine. You simply stopped eating, preferring all of your daily supplements and nutrients from a bottle and a capsule of vitamins. Your eyes were bloated and your bones protruded through your crisp, jaundiced skin.

Your mother is tending the weeds in her garden. 'Your father wouldn't want them,' she says. Your friend drives past in his big red tractor, going up the housing scheme. 'I've got a field up here,' he states, 'I'm going to grow whisky, then move to California.' 'Can you grow whisky?' I ask. 'Of course you can,' he answers, 'with barley sprouts.' The river flows past, with dead salmon floating on top. There's a deserted old studio. You walk towards it. Inside, it is designed like your degree show. She's standing there. 'I do art now too,' she says, 'I drew these for you.' They are black squiggles and splashes on white plates. 'They're like the pieces you created for your brother. Remember? How is he?' she asks. The people around you speak German. Your gallerist wheels up. 'Is your mum coming? She'll love it here.' It's cold. Why is Los Angeles so cold? I can't find her. I can't find Mum anywhere. She promised she would come to the show, with Dad and Gerald.

You visited my new set-up to console me. You were visibly shocked by my appearance. You wept, cursed at me, then flushed everything down the toilet.

'You're going to kill yourself. Is that what you want? Do you want to die too? What would that prove?' you say, exasperated.

I left the flat and wandered the city. I found myself at the wrong side of the Albert Bridge, in a dew-ringed dawn light, staring over towards our home. I took a taxi ride through the city, past Saint Paul's, down into the East End, to Hackney, and then to the south of the river. I came back to the loft apartment at nine in the morning sober, to find you asleep in a chair with half a cup of cold coffee by your side. I took you through to the bed with me and then collapsed. You nursed me for six days and nights. I was so ill I thought I might die. You left for two days then returned again. You were distant, warm, comforting, confrontational, sympathetic, and angry. I was too tired to leave the mattress. A few days later you left again for good. You advised me you would visit a solicitor to enact financial parity over the flat in Chelsea. I told you to just keep it for yourself.

I cry out to you in the dark. You are in the corner crying or laughing, I can't tell. You ask if I've eaten. I tell you I need to shit, but can't make it. Are you naked by the window? Are you masturbating? I can smell perfume, it's yours. I'm going to pee here.

I am carnage. I am solitude. Die, bastard die. What hope is there to carry on? All was lost long ago. The soul transported itself into the art. Some pieces of substance scrawled across another piece of substance, then bartered and traded, dismantled, forgotten and decayed. I am art.

My days were spent annihilated by consciousness. I fell into Soho cinemas and watched movies I cared nothing for. I galloped through galleries, disinterested in anything anyone had to offer. I ate bowls of soup and omelette frites, spicy chicken wraps and pulled-pork rolls, dim sum and sushi, washed down with gallons of wine: Spanish, French, Italian, Argentinian, New Zealand, Australian, Californian. I swallowed every painkiller I could press onto my tongue. I lay on the mattress watching tacky pornography and reality shows until I couldn't tell the difference anymore. I stopped relating to humanity. I bought a big television and a games console I couldn't even operate. I began to refer to the loft apartment and studio as my bunker complex. In my most delusional moments I began to identify with Hitler himself and Colonel Kurtz in *Apocalypse Now*.

The floor of the studio stretches on forever, into a purgatorial infinity. The sound of copulating couples rings all around, pulsating from the walls. I walk naked across the concrete floor; black painted footprints are left behind in my wake. I watch myself lying on a soiled mattress, my fingernails are missing. Little black wormlike creatures crawl out of my fingertips. I start to peel long flakes of my skin and lay them carefully on the floor. My stomach is distended and blotched with purple stains. I begin crying for no reason, claiming internally that they're all stolen. You are in the corner texting.

You pull out your right breast and begin to photograph it with a polaroid camera. 'It's the best way of taking a selfie,' you say from somewhere in the room which I cannot see. You squirt yellow pus from your nipple and scrape it off with your phone.

My LA gallerist had completed her renovation of the industrial-sized complex in North London and wished me to inaugurate its opening with the previously promised exhibition. She commanded from me a new centrepiece to be surrounded by former triumphs gathered from around the globe. I swallowed a ton of amphetamines, hired half a dozen people, set to work with drawings, sketches and paintings, and behold: another abortion is born. The completed works would be hung on giant canvases produced on site and with the title: *All the Heroes*. It was composed of each idol subsequently merging into the next to form a final, immense portrait of Christ. The figures included Ghandi, Martin Luther King, Karl Marx, Lenin, Chairman Mao, Emmeline Pankhurst, Nelson Mandela, Tito, James Connolly, Che Guevara, Simón Bolívar, Castro, Patrice Lumumba, Garbaldi, and Danton. They were deliberately staged to cause maximum controversy; nobody would be pleased, except for the gallery and the dealers. The work was completed in record time, with the ample aid of copious amounts of cocaine. I personally presented and dedicated the final work of Christ to the gallery owner. It was my final salvo of sarcasm to the art world. It was completely misunderstood and overlooked, of course.

She came to you in the dead of night. You were drunk on champagne and high on ecstasy. It was immediately obvious, even in your incapacitated state, that she was heavily pregnant. Her opening gambit was the declaration that the child belonged to you. You never reached sobriety at a quicker pace in your life. Her conscience had sent her. She didn't know how many opportunities she may have had in life left to get pregnant, so she was seizing that one wholeheartedly. She demanded nothing from you, but believed it was only correct that you were informed of the situation. Your response was to vomit in the sink. She made a weak joke in return. You had never considered ever becoming a parent. You were at a loss to any reasoned and rational response to your new position in the world. The baby was healthy and was a boy. Her mother was going to fly over from New Zealand closer to the due date and assist her for the initial few weeks after the birth. You were crippled by incapacity. You clumsily invited her to the preview for your retrospective a few days hence. She graciously accepted and left in a taxi home to Chelsea.

'It's okay. You don't need to do anything. You can play a role if you want, of course, but I'm not asking for anything from you. I'll find a way to support the child myself,' you said benevolently.

'I'll help, of course I will,' I stumbled out.

I spent the next thirty-six hours staring at blank walls, projecting my unborn child's life upon them. I couldn't imagine such a thing. It was a howl of insanity, the whole misadventure. I drastically packed a bag then took a cab to St Pancras station and left on a train for the Continent. I sat in the carriage pulling out of the station and as I left London for the final time, I realised I had been happy there in my own way. It was the place I would always most closely associate with myself and my life.

The desert landscape is calm and brutal. There is no wildlife yet appeared to greet the rising dawn. The herdsmen's slumber is coming to an end, the cattle will begin to low. The approaching sun will warm the earth and ravage all of its occupants, harrying them into the passive shade.

I moved under the ground of that great timeless paradise of debauchery, Paris, and sped my way down through rural

France past Bordeaux and on into Spain, to its fierce beating heart, Madrid. The warmth increased exponentially until I found myself in a muggy dawn on a large metropolitan railway platform. On the concourse some flamboyant character, who resembled a pimp, was shooting snaps of some barely-clad women that may well have been his clients.

My course of trajectory in Spain was completely unknown to me. I bagged a room in a modest hotel and relocated to the Prado.

You searched for her there. You searched for her all over the Madrid you had both known. Where you slept, where you ate, the meandering journeys you took through the city. You wanted her there and then, more than all of the others, including the mother of your child. How would it have played out? It was only going to end in one way and you knew it. You did nothing at the time to prevent it and there was nothing left to do then.

It felt so long ago that I had known you. I wrapped myself in a tartan blanket with a bottle of Highland malt in my hand and dreamt you back into the room and into my life. We could disappear now, over the sea that borders and into a hundred different territories, all new to us. We could live wild on the savannah, in a village on the edge of the desert; we could build an animal sanctuary, you always loved them at the zoo and wanted to free them. They could be free there, we could all be free there. My mother was dead. The woman who had given me life had died alone in her bed. I never even attended the funeral. I couldn't bury her, I couldn't bury any of them. All of their possessions went to charity. I have nothing of them. I have nothing of anyone. A woman, now a stranger too, grows my child inside of her. What connection do I have to anything? The umbilical cord harnesses those two together, it will always bind them.

I informed my solicitor to construct a will that left all my worldly possessions to her and all of my artistic estate to my unborn child. I kept a single edition of everything I ever produced and stored it in a top-security vault in Surrey. I always kept one step ahead of those thieving cunts in the art market and now my son could reap the rewards. It remains my belief that when it comes to the art world it is best to sleep with one eye open and a pistol under the pillow.

The stinging sand of the surrounding desert cannot penetrate him anymore. He is death exposed to life unilluminated. He will perish with the soil, scattered into the hemisphere. The earth he lies in will one day no longer exist. The light of the sun will be but a distant murmur at the other end of the universe. A luminance merely recorded by time and no longer by life.

Is the creation of art a recording of an existence? Can I prove incontrovertibly, through my art, that I lived? That I was a man? That I was here? That I passed through this world? Is that all decided instead through the genetics of another being? One who is me, but is not me. Will he know me through my art? What will he say of me? How could I teach him anything when I never even discovered any worthwhile knowledge myself?

I contacted a video artist I had known back in London who worked within the harsh landscapes of Southern Spain. He was living in social housing on the outskirts of the city. He was drug-dependent and had been dropped by his gallery. At the time he was writing a novel about an artist investigating the fraud of his own work and a network of international criminals. It sounded familiar territory to me. He claimed writing was easier than filming, and that it was more lucrative. He lived with his girlfriend, who waited bars. I spent a few days with him at his home. We chatted about art and politics, watched some La Liga football, and injected morphine together.

'The thing about the Spanish is, they're very spiritual

creatures. They're a bit like you Celts. When they love, they love forever; and when they hate, they hate all the way into the grave,' he stated enigmatically to me one afternoon in a state of narcotic repose.

'I don't understand.' Was all I could manage in response.

He had a great supply of the drug from someone who worked as an orderly at a hospital. When he could get hold of the cash for it he purchased the top-grade shit; this treat was on me. I had never taken anything intravenously before. He pulled the tourniquet on and shot me up, before doing so for himself. I wondered if I might die. If we would both pass out into another cold, dark world and his girlfriend would return from a heavy shift to find two corpses in her living room.

I found her infinite screaming endlessly fascinating. It entered into the flowery patterns on the wall. The television droned on in Spanish, I didn't care. I didn't think I would mind about anything ever again. How long was I there? Four days? We shot up another once and then for some reason left. We all took the train down to Seville. Her brother was in a band and he was playing a gig down there. We stayed in some anarchist squat, drank tequila, and smoked a lot of marijuana straight in from Mexico. I hooked up with some strange cats that seemed to be part of a cult. The leader was some creepy Jesus-type freak, with a long beard, long thinning hair, and uncut dirty fingernails. From what I could discern he was fucking all the girls in the group. He said they were all members of a folk circus band. I didn't know what that meant and neither did they. One of his brood, as he called them, said that he held her in thrall through black magic. I vacated with them to the Tabernas desert and ate peyote. I got lost, I got sick, I got sunburned, I got robbed of all my money, and then I eventually got a lift to Almeria.

'I'm going to haunt you to the grave,' he says conspiratorially in my ear, 'then I'll own your soul. You have forsaken it. You have forsaken me.' 'We're all forsaken,' says one of his girls as he fornicates with her. I see you in the dunes. You come towards me. 'Look,' you tell me, 'I've had a child with my mother. Do you want to see?' It is a photograph of me as a baby. I begin screaming, but no sounds present themselves. Written in the sand are the words '*Los Elos*'. I tell myself it means the group of the wolves. I ask him if I am a loupe? 'You're nothing. You're dead,' he says, 'we're all mort.'

After talking to my friend I briefly considered writing a book myself called: *A Memoir*. I bought a leather-bound notebook and some pens from a stationer's, and sat at a desk in the hotel. Nothing came. I sketched a vase of flowers instead. I had nothing to say. The words I had were gone. I bought a ticket instead from Algeciras to Ceuta.

You floated aimlessly south to Marrakesh. Fell in with some ex-pat foodie crowd that were discovering the delights of Moroccan cuisine, to export back to London in the form of street food. There were a few serious people you met, one of whom had seen your recent retrospective show.

'Well, if it isn't the great Douglas O'Connor. Imagine meeting you here. Your London exhibition is the best show of the year, man. It's a sensation. They're all wondering why you never showed up. Somebody said you had overdosed on morphine.'

'I did. Didn't anyone tell you? I'm dead. I died in the desert in Andalusia. I just haven't accepted it yet.'

You disappeared again soon after that on a train to the interior; to the Atlas mountains. You wanted to see hills again, like you had in Andalusia, so different from those at home. And then it dawned on you to remove yourself to a pre-birth era.

The land and the sky and the stars stretched on for eternity across an empty and desolate earth. Through sandstorms and blistering heat I lost all sense of time and place and memory. I arrived at I know not where. I got sick along the way. I recognise nothing anymore.

He groans helplessly as the land begins to rise once more with the coming of dawn. All that have survived the night will live for one more day. The animals and people now begin to stir. Nothing can be left to chance in such a cruel and hostile climate.

He is death incarnate beneath his burial clothes. A corpse tipping towards oblivion on the edge of the universe.

The light draws itself up; a warm pink glow, gleaming on the horizon from the east, as the sun rises over the continent which gave birth to the dawn of life and I am left here, prostate and alone, watching the fragments floating off into the abyss.

Thanks for reading. If you have enjoyed *Memories From the End of the World,* and have a spare moment, would you consider leaving a review on the book's Amazon page?

As well as being very gratifying for the author, a positive review is really helpful for other readers in deciding whether or not they might enjoy a book. For independent authors in particular, it can be very hard work building a readership so your positive review may be instrumental in helping to build a successful writing career.

The Painter by Ewen MacDonald

'He held the detached tooth in front of his face. It was white and cracked, with roots dangling beneath, festering in gore... then he placed the tooth back into his mouth and rolled it around, before swallowing it whole.'

The Painter awakes naked and injured. Where are his clothes, what is his name, and, more importantly, why is the chair talking to him?

So begins The Painter's disquieting journey into the heart of darkness at the centre of the contemporary art world.

After suffering a traumatic epiphany, The Painter turns his back on his former existence and becomes a living artwork. His life is his canvas, his materials bodily matters and fluids. His creations are the remnants of all he tastes, touches and feels.

But how will those who feed off his talent feel about this change?

As the corpses mount up, their tableaux ever more macabre, the finger begins to point inexorably in The Painter's direction. Pitted against amoral art collectors, corrupt critics and homicidal gangsters, his sole ally is a beautiful young gallerist, who has her own demons to wrestle.

The Painter is Raymond Chandler meets Francis Bacon in purgatory.

www.ingramcontent.com/pod-product-compliance
Lightning Source LLC
Chambersburg PA
CBHW031153020426
42333CB00013B/636